TEIKYO WESTMAR UN

CHARLES ROSEN is a pianist whose cele-
brated concert career spans many decades and
continents, and whose notable recordings over
a wide range of the piano repertory have been
awarded many accolades. He was the Charles
Eliot Norton Professor at Harvard University
in 1980–81, and is now a professor of music
and social thought at the University of Chicago.
His first book, *The Classical Style*, won the
National Book Award in 1972; he is a frequent
contributor to *The New York Review of Books*.

Jacket design by Michael Ian Kaye
Jacket art by Leslie Schiff
Author photograph by Catherine Temerson

Hill and Wang
A division of Farrar, Straus and Giroux
19 Union Square West
New York 10003

THE FRONTIERS OF MEANING

THE ANNUAL NEW YORK REVIEW OF BOOKS

AND

HILL AND WANG

LECTURE SERIES

Series No. 1
given in Rome at the Conservatorio Santa Cecilia
on March 28, 29, and 30, 1993

THE FRONTIERS OF MEANING

THE ANNUAL NEW YORK REVIEW OF BOOKS

AND

HILL AND WANG

LECTURE SERIES

Series No. 1
given in Rome at the Conservatorio Santa Cecilia
on March 28, 29, and 30, 1993

ALSO BY CHARLES ROSEN

The Classical Style: Haydn, Mozart, and Beethoven

Arnold Schönberg

Sonata Forms

The Musical Languages of Elliott Carter

Romanticism and Realism:
The Mythology of Nineteenth-Century Art
(WITH HENRI ZERNER)

Plaisir de Jouer, Plaisir de Penser
(WITH CATHERINE TEMERSON)

THE
FRONTIERS
OF MEANING

THREE INFORMAL LECTURES
ON MUSIC

CHARLES ROSEN

 HILL AND WANG

A DIVISION OF FARRAR, STRAUS AND GIROUX

New York

94-1924

Copyright © 1994 by Charles Rosen
All rights reserved
Printed in the United States of America
Published simultaneously in Canada by HarperCollins*CanadaLtd*
Designed by Fritz Metsch
First edition, 1994

LIBRARY OF CONGRESS CATALOGING-IN-PUBLICATION DATA
Rosen, Charles.
The frontiers of meaning : three informal lectures on music /
Charles Rosen.— 1st ed.

p.   cm.
Includes index.
1. Music—Philosophy and aesthetics. 2. Music—History and
criticism. I. Title.
ML3845.R68   1994   781'.1—dc20   93-39614   CIP   MN

"Picking and Choosing," from *The Complete Poems of
Marianne Moore* by Marianne Moore. Copyright © 1981 by
Clive E. Driver, Literary Executor of the Estate of Marianne
Moore. Used by permission of Viking Penguin, a division of
Penguin Books USA Inc.

FOR

DAVID JAMES

CONTENTS

PREFACE

THE FIRST and third of these three talks are about some of the ways that music appears to have a meaning although it does not transmit a message. The approach is indirect; it is important to avoid the common fallacy that there is a secret code that we have to learn in order to understand music. There is no code, secret or otherwise: we do not have access to a dictionary of musical significance. As we learn, largely unconsciously, how musical composition works within a given tradition, we understand how music can refer outside itself to a whole culture and civilization of which it is a small part. The second lecture attempts to dispel some of the myths about how that tradition is formed.

The lectures were given in Rome in March 1993, at the invitation of Hill and Wang, *The New York Review of Books*, and *La Rivista dei Libri*. I have revised the text slightly but have not changed their characters or basic form. The third lecture in particular was conceived in terms of the musical examples that were played.

I am very grateful to Rae Hederman, publisher

of *The New York Review of Books*, for his great kindness, and for his making it possible to give the lectures in Rome under such agreeable conditions. The editor of *La Rivista dei Libri*, Pietro Corsi, provided all kinds of practical help and good company as well. I am indebted to Dr. Kristina Muxfeldt above all for help with the pages on Schubert, to Henri Zerner for advice and moral support, and to Elisabeth Sifton for sensibly removing so many awkward turns of phrase. Scott Griffin and Abigail Cheever are owed thanks for helping me put the lectures in printable shape. Last but foremost I am grateful to Robert Silvers for his counsel, his suggestions, and his encouragement.

C.R.

THE FRONTIERS OF MEANING

1

THE FRONTIERS OF NONSENSE

WHAT DOES it mean to understand music? It is easy enough to explain or define if one starts at the most modest level. Understanding music simply means not being irritated or puzzled by it. When, at the age of seventeen, I heard the Fifth Quartet of Béla Bartók (the first long work of that composer I had ever encountered), it made me physically sick; I remember quite clearly a feeling of nausea. My lack of familiarity with the style meant that everything I expected of music was frustrated and thwarted, and the quartet was just close enough to the kind of music I knew and loved best for the frustrations to be particularly painful. Today, of course, the Fifth Quartet gives me nothing but pleasure—with, occasionally, a slight sense of disappointment because of my overfamiliarity with the piece as well as its style: it no longer solicits my attention at every turn as it once did.

More positively, taking pleasure in music is the most obvious sign of comprehension, the proof that we understand it, and we may extend that to sympathy with other listeners' enjoyment—at least if a work that I used to play, like the Third Piano Sonata of Hindemith, no longer gives me pleasure, I am not bewildered by someone else's pleasure: I once shared it.

It is not, however, the unfamiliarity or strangeness of a work or of a composer's manner that is a bar to understanding, but rather the disappearance of the familiar, the ongoing disappointment of the expectations and hopes fostered by the musical tradition in which we have grown up. Not novelty, therefore, but the absence of something recognizable in its style, its language—something we once thought essential to music—makes listening to a radically original work a test we are likely to fail. I waited in vain to hear in the Bartók quartet a symmetry of phrasing and a resolution of harmony that I thought all music had to have and that the music refused to grant. Leo Steinberg once cleverly pointed out that resistance to the great masters of early-twentieth-century modernist painting did not come from what they put into the pictures but from what they left out. Abstraction at first shocked us because we believed that painting should represent nature. When we got used to the absence of natural shapes, we could admire the equilibrium of forms and the virtuoso brushwork. Later, the revolutionary technique of some of the members of the New York school would not permit us the pleasure in brushwork, and we had to learn to admire the dramatic gestures of paint thrown or dripped onto the canvas—only to be frustrated once again by the hard-edged style of Ellsworth Kelly and Roy Lichtenstein, where the smooth surfaces looked impersonal and even self-consciously commercial, and we at first refused to admit that it could be art. In music, the loss of tonality was deeply upsetting, no matter how much the history of nineteenth-century music seemed to lead to it, at least in hindsight, but we learned to take pleasure in the passionate phrasing of Schönberg and Berg. The coolness, the apparent absence of passion of Anton von Webern was the next obstacle to overcome, but we were won over by the exquisite balance of his symmetrical patterns—only to have these subsequently withheld by younger composers influenced by Webern, like Pierre Boulez, who substituted a much more freewheeling texture.

We can, in fact, relive the history of taste in our own lives, the way embryos are supposed to go through the history of the evolution of a species. I am told, although I do not remember this myself, that at the age of eight I was made indignant by my first hearing of Debussy. There should be a law against music like that, I am supposed to have declared roundly. This was understandable enough: my favorite composers were Wagner and Beethoven. The influence of Wagner on Debussy and the logic with which Debussy continued the Wagnerian tradition in new ways were as incomprehensible to me as they were to most of Debussy's contemporaries. The normal reaction to music we do not understand is moral outrage, and I was quite ready to have music that I did not yet understand proscribed and banned.

If getting used to music is the essential condition for understanding, it is hard to see just what purpose is served by writing about it. A few experiences of listening to a symphony or nocturne are worth more than any essay or analysis. The work of art itself teaches us how to understand it, and makes the critic not merely parasitical but strictly superfluous. This is not an unprecedented dilemma but one in which the critic of literature found himself at the end of the eighteenth century, when the function of criticism as an act of judgment crumbled before his eyes. The accepted criteria that had served so well for centuries began to seem the heritage of an alien culture; it no longer required any courage, or provoked any surprise, to question the authority of the classics, and it became almost commonplace to assume that the models given by Homer, Virgil, and Horace were no longer relevant to the literature of contemporary Europe. With the realization that absolute standards were not valid for new civilizations and different cultures, critics were compelled to derive their measures of evaluation from each culture in turn, and then from each individual author, and finally from each work. Standards could no longer be imposed from outside or in advance, and critics finally recognized that a new work was capable of establishing its own system of values. Here is the basis for Wordsworth's famous affirmation that an original poet "must himself create the taste by which he is to be relished." The more traditional, straightforward exercise of judgment was left to journalists. Critical evaluation was transformed into understanding, and criticism became not an act of judgment but of comprehension.*

This is the legacy of Romanticism, and critics who would like to maintain or return to absolute standards have been protesting it without much success for almost two centuries. Whether there is, in fact, anything constant or invariant about aesthetic appreciation is irrelevant—even if there is, it must be on a level of such generality that it can never

---

* A remarkably explicit statement of the new attitude to criticism was made by the French historian Prosper de Barante, best known for his *History of the Dukes of Burgundy* (1824–26), in which he introduced into medieval history a picturesque sense of local color derived from the novels of Walter Scott. Toward the beginning of his essay on the life of Friedrich Schiller (written in 1821), he writes:

. . . there is no question here of subjecting Schiller's productions to certain rules, comparing them to forms one has a taste for and is accustomed to, and finding them good or bad; anyone can decide about this in his own way. To indulge in such an examination would be a superfluous and sterile task. On the contrary, there may

help us in any given instance. Our sensuous appreciation of the world and of the works created by man has, no doubt, a biological foundation, one shared by all human beings, but that is no use to us when we try to evaluate a Bach fugue or a Dostoevsky novel—or even the simple experience of a landscape, as our delight in the view of a mountain or a waterfall is also determined by the traditions of our culture. The coexistence of different criteria of judgment is, in any case, by now a fact of life. Beethoven cannot be judged or even understood by the standards of Mozart, however much he may have continued them, nor Berg by the standards of Wagner or Richard Strauss, nor Elliott Carter by the values of Ives and Stravinsky. A work of music can be only partially integrated into history, although that partial integration may be inescapable: it also

> be some advantage in studying the relation of Schiller's works to the character, situation and opinions of the author, and with the circumstances surrounding him. Criticism, conceived thus, does not have so facile and absolute a character as when it absolves or condemns a work according to its greater or lesser resemblance to given forms; but it approaches more closely to the study of man and to that observation of the progressive development of the human spirit, the most useful and the most curious of all studies.[1]

There are other statements of the way in which literary critics rejected the act of judgment as superfluous and a bar to original creation, but none clearer.

demands to be listened to as if nothing had come before it and nothing was to come afterward.

The paradox was stated explicitly in that manifesto of Central European Romanticism first published in 1799, the *Athenaeum*, at the beginning of the section of book reviews:

> Excellent works generally criticize [characterize, or review] themselves, and in this respect it is superfluous for another to perform yet again the very task that the author has doubtless already done. If such a criticism, nevertheless, is a work of art (as it always ought to be), then its existence is anything but superfluous; but it stands entirely for itself and is as independent of the written work criticized as this itself is independent of the material treated and described within it.[2]

This proclaims the independence of the critic, which may here be equated with the freedom of the artist; and it must be recognized that a small degree of irresponsibility is necessary for a critic with any self-respect. Without that irresponsibility the work of criticism is indeed superfluous. If the principles of judgment are to be drawn from the work of art itself, it is clear that its creator has already done that, even if only implicitly. Understanding will arise more effectively by rereading or relistening than by having someone else repeat the artist's work for him, an experience that will inevitably be less authentic and probably less convincing. The critic is then left with the act of interpretation—and this only if interpretation is understood as a creative and original act, at the very least a reshaping of the work before our eyes.

This proclamation of critical independence, which set out firmly enough in 1799 the task of criticism for the next two centuries, continues a paragraph later to suggest that one further critical activity can be granted a full right to exist: the clearing away of possible misunderstandings, or the translation of a work written in an esoteric dialect or jargon into a language understandable by the lay reader. Either creative interpretation, then, or *explication de texte*: what in music we call analysis, justifiable only when it removes misreading or some kind of error of perception. Analysis for its own sake was not envisaged by Friedrich Schlegel, the probable author of the passage I have been quoting, but perhaps he would not have been surprised to learn that it has become a basic academic industry in modern times, as its similarity to the professional exercise of biblical exegesis, then publicly supported by the university, would have been evident enough.

In any case, besides the grand task of interpretation, in which his imagination could take free flight, the critic had the more mundane responsibility of making it possible for the public to assimilate the unfamiliar, to translate the esoteric into everyday language. Familiarity has its dangers, however, particularly when it allows us to settle comfortably into error—the name generally given to widely accepted error is *tradition*. In musical performance practice, tradition is the way we have been playing the music, more often wrong than right, for the past twenty years. The influence of long-ingrained habit upon our conception of music is especially interesting when it is ambiguous, that is, when we are not certain whether the habit is deeply mistaken or not. This uncovers the hidden bias in our unconscious expectations.

Marianne Moore wrote, in her poem "Picking and Choosing":

> *We are not daft about the meaning,*
> *but this familiarity with wrong meanings*
> *puzzles one . . .*

Wrong meanings? Music always hovers on the edge of the meaningless, of nonsense. As I have said, understanding music largely means feeling comfortable with it; the music conforms to our expectations of musical grammar and syntax, and we are then able to attach a meaning to it partly by tradition (slow music in the minor mode is often melancholy, for example), and partly, it must be said, by caprice, by the free use of our imagination. The wonderfully silly belief of some commentators, for example, that the Baroque dotted rhythms represent the waves of the Rhine in Schumann's setting of Heine's poem about the cathedral at Cologne ("On the Rhine, the holy stream" in *Dichterliebe*) is merely free association, backed up by the unwarranted conviction that a song must always illustrate, not the general sense, but the opening line of its lyric—no Romantic composer believed that a river flows with the jagged rhythm of a French overture.

All is well as long as the unfamiliar work does not break with what we think is the proper grammatical structure of music, the correct resolution of dissonance, the familiar placing of the cadence, the expected balance of the melodic phrase. When the composer violates the traditional musical language in order to re-create part of it in his own way, the public must learn the new form of expression, become familiar with it, listen to it often enough to feel comfortable with it. But what happens when we are uncertain whether the incomprehensible is an innovation or a mistake, a new creation or a misprint? At the first performance of Stravinsky's *Apollon Musagète*, I am told, the conductor decided that many of Stravinsky's dissonances must have been mistakes of the copyist, and replaced them with blander harmonies.

Normally, misprints are either easily corrected or else so trivial that it makes no difference whether we play the correct or the faulty version. Beethoven claimed that many of the dynamic indications in the first printing of his three piano sonatas opus 31 were badly placed, and most of these mistaken indications are easy enough to correct—although, unfortunately, few musicians are sensitive enough to Beethoven's idiosyncratic use of dynamics to be bothered by the wrong ones. In any case, a sure way of getting some of the details wrong would be to follow the original printed score pedantically and faithfully.

Nevertheless, on rare occasions, a misprint or slip of the pen may challenge our view of the musical language. These extreme cases may help us understand a little more about the way music acquires meaning, or what it means to say that the music makes sense. We may take as an example the famous and controversial A-sharp in the first movement of Beethoven's *Hammerklavier* Sonata, opus 106, that monument of late classicism which asserted the composer's right to disregard the desires and needs of the musical amateur. Here is how it was printed in the original publications, Viennese as well as English; the place is just before the beginning of the recapitulation:

There are certainly many mistakes among the accidentals in the first editions of Beethoven's works. The manuscript of the *Hammerklavier* is lost, but it is not sure that finding it would help us: Beethoven was quite capable of making mistakes in manuscript, as well as in reading proof.

[14]

The initial reaction to this passage was that Beethoven had forgotten to indicate an A-natural, and it was accordingly changed in most subsequent editions. But original reactions are not always trustworthy. As witness we may remember the distaste of the early-nineteenth-century conservative French critic François-Joseph Fétis for the beautiful sustained E-flat in the clarinet in this passage from the slow movement of Beethoven's Symphony No. 5:

To Fétis's unimaginative mind (his admirers claim that he had his virtues, but they pale beside his incomprehension of Beethoven, Berlioz, Wagner, and almost anyone else in his century) this dissonance could only be a misprint, and the clarinet must follow the melody in the lower voice and rise to an F for two bars:

This rightfully earned him the contempt of Berlioz, who fought for the correct original reading. (The impossibility of Fétis's emendation is revealed at once by the disagreeable awkwardness of the hidden parallel octaves that result.) Fétis's attempt to turn Beethoven's inspiration into something conventional obliquely illustrates the cogency in fields other than philology of an important and long-established principle of the interpretation and emendation of classical Latin and Greek texts: the superiority of the "difficult reading," the version that requires justification, stimulates thought, causes surprise, disrupts our set ways of thought.

The preference for the difficult reading has created the controversy about the *Hammerklavier*'s A-sharp. The A-natural is only too obvious both to the ear and to the mind: it is the note we would expect. In our century, modernism and the hope of establishing a difficult reading have naturally given rise to the adventurous project of justifying the A-sharp. That is not as difficult as it might seem at first sight, although the dissonance it creates has few precedents in the kind of formal context where it occurs—a passage that sets up the return of the tonic and of the main theme. The A-sharp and the tritone it produces imply not the tonic, B-flat major, but B major. However, not only does the development section just before this retransition end in B major but Beethoven almost immediately brings back the dominant of B major for an extensive development, ending with an astonishing climax in B minor. It is not impossible that Beethoven allowed the return of B-flat major to be influenced both by the extraordinary B major ending of the development section and by the even more extraordinary appearance of B minor at the most powerful climax in the movement:

Some years ago, a distinguished Austrian pianist told me that he rejects the A-sharp because it robs the traditional, climactic return of the tonic B-flat major of its force and its grand sonority, but that actually misses the point: whether or not the A-sharp is correct, this B-flat major climax is unquestionably intended to be inferior in power and emotional force to the B minor explosion that will come later, as an examination of the texture and pedal indications shows.

The same prejudice in favor of a grand climax at

the return of the tonic at the opening of the recapitulation caused nineteenth-century editors to add
absolutely unauthorized octaves to this tonic return:

This serves mainly to show how pianists used to
think Beethoven ought to have scored this return if
only he had a more modern idea of piano technique,
but in addition it betrays the conventional assumption that the beginning of the recapitulation, with
the return of the main theme and of the tonic harmony, should be the occasion of a big climax and
a loud noise.

There is also a sketch for the disputed passage
that would indicate an A-natural instead of the
A-sharp, but the sketch is very different from the
final version, and does not carry complete conviction. Everyone would admit that the A-natural is
part of the expected progression: the question is,
did Beethoven rework the conventional harmony in
this passage to reflect the unique character of the
first movement as a whole? The amount of revision
to which Beethoven subjected his most surprising

[18]

effects was often considerable, as we can see from Lewis Lockwood's recent study of the sketches for the equally astonishing entry of the horn with the wrong harmony just before the recapitulation of the first movement of the *Eroica* Symphony.[3] Little minds in the nineteenth century also thought the horn entry must be a mistake; even smaller minds in the twentieth thought it a joke. We may conclude that the moment before the return of the opening theme in the tonic was a place for some of Beethoven's most curious and outrageous violations of traditional harmony.

Donald Francis Tovey concluded, I think correctly, that the A-sharp in the *Hammerklavier* was indeed a mistake but that Beethoven would have been delighted with it if he had noticed it. This may sound like a facetious suggestion, but it is nothing of the kind. Beethoven's correspondence with his publisher about the scherzo of his Sonata for Piano and Cello opus 69 reveals this possibility amusingly enough. The fortissimo on the second note of the melody excited Beethoven's correction:

In the very first bar, the *ff* should be removed. Afterward . . . the *ff* should again be removed and *p* should be inserted for the very first note, and similarly the second time the key signature changes, the *ff* should be removed.

[19]

This, from a letter of July 26, 1809, to Breitkopf und Härtel, is decisive enough. Five days later we have:

> Laugh over my author's anxiety. Imagine, I find that yesterday, in correcting the errors in the violoncello sonata, I myself made new errors. So, in the scherzo allegro molto, let this *ff* remain at the very beginning just the way it was indicated, and also the other times. [A marginal note adds: That is, the way it stood in the first place is correct.]

Which letter are we to believe? The manuscript of the scherzo is lost, and the principle that the last decision of the composer is to be followed will not, I think, help us here, but some conclusions from Beethoven's other works can enlighten us. The sudden fortissimo is, in fact, a very Beethovenian detail—and that is the problem. What follows from the dramatic accent does not fit any other work of Beethoven: that is, nothing follows from it. If it had been in Beethoven's original conception of the theme, there would have been some development of the idea, but there is none, merely a literal repetition of the effect each time the scherzo begins again (and it is clear that Beethoven did not write out the scherzo each time, but merely directed the engraver to repeat the opening section as indicated the first time). An explosive accent in the first bar of the initial motif is not a detail that Beethoven would have ignored for the rest of the movement. The cello never participates in the effect, and, most important, the fortissimo has no consequences in the rest of the scherzo.

I think that Beethoven's initial rejection of the marking was correct but that the more he looked at the misprint, the more he was taken with it, seduced by its dramatic character. We have here an entertaining case of familiarity gradually convincing even the composer of the correctness of an error. It took only a few days' consideration for Beethoven to persuade himself that the mistake could be given a meaning, that it made sense after all.

In the same way, what looks at first sight like a misprint in the *Hammerklavier* turns out to have a musical interest after all, not merely as a local effect but even in the structure as a whole. That is why so many intelligent pianists have been seduced by it. My own position is that the A-sharp is probably a misprint: it is so radical a harmonic effect that one might think that Beethoven would have called attention to it by adding an accidental to the spot, not merely relying upon the key signature to do its conventional work. There is, however, a small chance that it was intended by Beethoven; it is musically more interesting and even superior to the A-natural that is probably correct; I have been playing the more dubious A-sharp for years and will continue to do so. It is the moral duty of a performer to choose what he thinks is the musically superior version, whatever the composer's clearly marked intention—it is also the moral responsibility of a pianist to try to convince himself that the composer knew what he was doing. In this wonderfully powerful moment in opus 106 the moral issues have been happily clouded.

A gross error at the opening of Chopin's Sonata in B-flat Minor is even more interesting: in all twentieth-century editions, the repeat of the exposition is wrongly indicated to commence at the beginning of the fifth bar, when it should start with the first. I have already talked about this in some lectures to be published shortly, and even printed the relevant pages, so I will not rehearse all the arguments again here.[4] But I should like to cast an eye upon the acceptance of the mistake over a century and a half and the results of my attempt to rectify it—a tale in which a number of people, including myself, come out, amusingly, in a most unfavorable light. It will serve to clarify the way music acquires significance, and what makes it seem intelligible to listener and to performer.

To start with, I am by no means the only musician to have perceived the mistake and certainly not the first. The excellent Hungarian pianist Béla Siki, a pupil of Ernst von Dohnányi who now lives on the

West Coast, was aware of the mistake, and I remember discussing the point with him some years ago when I was playing in Cincinnati and he was teaching there. The passage was printed correctly by Johannes Brahms, who edited the sonatas late in the nineteenth century for the critical edition published by Breitkopf und Härtel, an edition reprinted after the Second World War for many years by Kalmus. I probably saw it and compared it with the standard editions of Chopin then in use by most pianists and most teachers: those edited by Rafael Joseffy, by Chopin's pupil Carl Mikuli, and the particularly interesting one by Karl Klindworth, an incomparable witness to the way the various fioriture in Chopin's music were articulated and phrased in the late nineteenth century. The conclusion that they were wrong and Brahms was right was not hard to reach.

The important thing to see is that the standard version is patently idiotic. Except for the fact that so many have believed it, I would have said that it is impossible to imagine that Chopin would have composed the modulation that results when one goes from the end of the exposition back to the fifth bar. Indeed, it ought to be impossible to believe that any professional musician wrote it, since it is literally incompetent. There is no way that Chopin—or anyone else—would proceed from an interrupted cadence on D-flat directly into the key of B-flat minor.

The chord of B-flat minor with which the fifth bar starts is remotely possible as a small detail of a longer progression, although it is exceedingly ineffective, and it would be unlike Chopin to spoil a remarkably dramatic moment in this way; to continue from that chord as if the key of B-flat minor had been genu-inely reestablished is out of the question. Here is the end of the exposition, followed by the opening six bars:

What I should like to consider is how the incompetent misplacement of the repeat could continue to be printed for more than a hundred and fifty years as the standard version.

The source of the error is the double bar at the beginning of the fifth measure, which is there simply to indicate a change of tempo: Chopin directs the pianist to go from an opening slow tempo (Grave) to double tempo, which amounts to a sudden Allegro. In reality, since the instruction to play twice as fast as before is meant to be taken literally and not freely (it is, after all, "Doppio movimento" and not "Più Allegro" that Chopin writes), there is no change of pulse, but only a change of notation. The only extant manuscript, a copy corrected by Chopin himself, clearly shows the double bar without the two dots that would direct a repeat to commence there. Three editions were published more or less simultaneously by Chopin, in Leipzig, Paris, and London. The Leipzig engraver mistakenly took the double bar for an indication of a repeat and added the dots. Most editors generally attach the highest authority to the Paris edition, as Chopin lived in that city, and sometimes corrected proofs; given the unanimous agreement of modern editors, I presumed that the error was repeated in the Paris printing. I looked at the London edition and found that it was correct—in fact, it not only lacks the erroneous dots that indicate a repeat but does not even have a double bar, although it clearly directs a change of tempo. The bibliographical evidence of the manuscript copy and the London edition should be confirmed by musical arguments, of course, which I set forth in my article, above all emphasizing the fact that the last two chords of the exposition each last as long as two full bars, clearly signifying that Chopin has returned to the half tempo of the opening Grave. It appears that Chopin had the original idea of beginning his sonata with the last note of the exposition and modulating into the tonic, a wonderfully effective device.

The English conductor Jeffrey Tate, with whom I discussed this issue, told the Japanese pianist Mitsuko Uchida about it; he has worked extensively with her, and she was about to record the sonata. I went backstage after one of her recitals to congratulate her, and she wanted to know what evidence I had on this matter. I felt that the musical evidence should have been sufficient, and it generally has been for most musicians with whom I have discussed it; but I told her about the evidence of the manuscript copy and the London edition. This turned out badly, as her recording, in which she started the repeat reasonably from bar 1, was attacked in France by a critic of *Le Monde de la Musique*, Alain Lompech: he complained that she seemed to be unable to read music and was evidently shocked by what he considered a novelty, or by the disruption of his habits of listening.

Shortly afterward, I played a public recital on the French radio of two sonatas of Chopin (not, however, the B-flat minor one, which I had performed under the same auspices the year before, but the Cello Sonata and the Sonata No. 3 for Piano). The recital was followed by a round-table discussion on Chopin at which M. Lompech was present, and another panel member had the unfortunate idea of bringing up my recently published article in *Nineteenth-Century Music*. M. Lompech indignantly demanded how I could explain that Chopin had not corrected the copy of the Paris edition of this sonata owned by his pupil Jane Stirling, now in the Bibliothèque Nationale. I replied that Jane Stirling was not known as a very brilliant pianist, that she certainly could not have played this sonata, and Chopin annotated only her copies of pieces she played for him. M. Lompech declared that she did play the B-flat minor sonata.

The matter might have rested there. Recently, however, I did what I should have done long before, and consulted the publication in facsimile by the Bibliothèque Nationale of all the pages of the Jane Stirling copy with annotations by Chopin, and found that indeed she had not played the whole B-flat minor sonata, for only pages from the relatively easy funeral march were annotated. The other three movements would clearly have been beyond her capacities. There were no annotations at all to the first movement.

Sometime later I received a call from Professor Jeffrey Kallberg of the University of Pennsylvania; his insight into Chopin's style is unsurpassed, he knows as much as any other scholar of nineteenth-century music about the texts of Chopin's music (there are probably no more than one or two others who know as much), and he has a kind and generous nature. "What makes you think that the Paris edition is incorrect?" he asked. I replied, somewhat embarrassed, that I had never actually bothered to look at that edition, but assumed that it was as incorrect as the Leipzig printing, since modern editions using it as a source and giving variant readings (including Henle and the infamous "Paderewski" edition) had never indicated otherwise. The reprise of the exposition in the Paris printing, Kallberg told me, starts correctly from the first bar, not the fifth. In short, even if Jane Stirling had played the movement, Chopin would not have needed to correct her copy.

The sloppiness of my research was only too evident; not to have consulted the major source easy of access before publishing an article on the subject is not something to be proud of. Kallberg's news, however, only added to the mystery why editors persist in printing the foolish indication at the fifth bar and showing no variant reading. Kallberg guessed they must have been following the Leipzig edition, but I do not think this is the case. When they claimed to have consulted the Paris edition and to give the variant readings, I think we must believe them. They did not see the correct reading because they were unable to recognize what was in front of their eyes; the "Paderewski" editors even printed a photograph of the manuscript in Warsaw without noticing that it has no indication of repetition at the fifth bar.

To explain why a reading that makes no sense was accepted unthinkingly by almost all nineteenth- and twentieth-century editors, including Chopin's own students, is not, in fact, very difficult. On paper, the first four bars, marked Grave, look like an introduction, since it is usual for an introduction to be in a slower tempo. Further, when there is a slow introduction, it is traditional to begin the repeat of the exposition with the arrival of the Allegro. Chopin's double bar at the change of tempo looks sufficiently like the usual notation for such a repeat to be mistaken for it. The tradition of playing the exposition of a sonata twice gradually fell into disuse in public concerts during the nineteenth century, to be revived in the mid-twentieth by musicians with an artistic conscience and pretensions to scholarship. Most of the pianists I have spoken to have

CHARLES ROSEN

tried out the repeat as printed in all twentieth-
century editions, discovered that it sounds terrible,
and decided to omit it. (This is a pity, as the first
movement is surprisingly short without the repeat,
and would gain from the extra weight.) For all these
reasons, it escaped notice that these bars are not,
strictly speaking, an introduction but, rather, one
of the two main themes that Chopin used throughout the central development section. In other words,
the opening motif in these four bars does not reap-
pear in the development as if it were something
outside the main body of the principal form—like
the surprising reappearance of the *Introduzione* in the
middle of the development section of Schumann's
Sonata for Piano in F-sharp Minor or like the return
of the Introduction at the beginning of the development section in Beethoven's *Pathétique* Sonata.*
Rather, the opening Grave motif is simply combined
with the other principal theme in the development
section, even fused with it, as part of the standard

* The contention, always passionately maintained by Rudolf
Serkin, that the first page of the *Pathétique*, too, is intended
to be replayed with the repeat of the exposition is a different
problem, as it neither creates nor avoids a compositional sole-
cism, and as the function of the opening slow section is not
ambiguous: it is clearly a traditional introduction. The only
musical question is whether or not the structure is more dramatic if one includes the introduction when repeating the
exposition, and enhances the parallelism of its return at the
opening of the development.

motivic process for a central development. It is, then, not a prologue but a separate principal motif. A four-bar cadence on the tonic is used first to establish that key from a chromatic distance and then, the second time around, to finish the interrupted cadence at the end of the exposition.

It also makes no sense to interpret these four opening bars in a free slow tempo, as they work when played again on the return only if the tempo is more or less exactly twice as slow as the succeeding tempo. Most pianists play these bars around four times as slowly as the succeeding "Doppio movimento," and then the relation between the two speeds ceases to have any meaning. Even more important, the final cadence of the exposition is, in fact, not completely resolved with the first bar of the return but only with the second, where the right hand reenters. If the pianist does not indicate his understanding that the upper note is a delayed melody note, the voice leading—always so important in Chopin—remains unrealized and the passage does not make its full point.

Editors are generally a humble lot: they work visually from the appearance of each detail, and ask not if it makes sense but only if it conforms to other details similar to it in the same piece or in the same tradition. The erroneous repeat sign at Chopin's fifth bar resembles the correct indication at the fifth bar of Beethoven's Sonata in F-sharp Major, opus 78, for example, and many other parallels could be adduced, like Beethoven's *Les Adieux* Sonata or Mozart's great Sonata in F Major for four hands. What is unusual in the case of Chopin's B-flat minor sonata is not so much that the misdirection is idiotic as that so many editors agreed in making the same error. Natural incompetence is no more widespread among musicologists than among plumbers, although the results are usually less immediately inconvenient. Other and equally foolish mistakes, however, are normally made on an individual basis.

Editorial originality is exercised most often in the interests of visual conformity. Editors want the musical text to look coherent, to regiment the details neatly. Wolfgang Boetticher, for example, who edited Robert Schumann's piano works for Henle, finds lots of ligatures tying two notes over a bar on one page of the Novelette No. 8, so he adds a tie between two E-naturals where it was missing:[5]

Here is Clara Schumann's edition of the same passage:

In Clara's Nocturne, from which this beautiful melody comes, the second note of the theme is never tied but always repeated, and Schumann repeats the note as well wherever he uses the melody in his novelette, but that does not deter Boetticher. All he can see is that the page looks typographically more uniform with another tie, so he puts it in.

In the Mazurkas of Chopin, also published by Henle, the editor, Ewald Zimmerman, observed, in a pupil's copy of the Mazurka in B Minor, opus 33, no. 4, two crosses in the composer's hand over the first two beats of the last bar, and he conjectured that this was Chopin's suggestion to omit these two beats. He is not discouraged by the fact that this would produce outright nonsense:

And he did not bother to find out that Chopin habitually scrawled crosses in students' copies to indicate approval of certain renditions. These errors are no less foolish than the repeat of the exposition in Chopin's Sonata in B-flat Minor, but they are individual inventions, not mass delusions.

The near unanimity of editors who persist in reproducing the mistake in the sonata's first movement must arise from something more than the way the notation makes the first phrase resemble a four-bar slow introduction to a principal Allegro. Margaret Bent (formerly of Princeton, now of All Souls, Oxford) pointed out to me that even Edward Cone began by defending the misprinted version—perhaps because of the challenge that a difficult reading gave him—and then changed his mind, observing that beginning with the first bar was "one solution" to the problem. This shows how far this distinguished and intelligent musician was troubled by years of familiarity with the wrong reading, since, in fact, returning to the first bar is the only solution; there is no other possibility, nor has anybody ever suggested one.

The agreement of so many editors through the

years on an absolutely senseless reading is a tribute to the originality of this passage, to its innovative nature: an introduction that turns out not to be an introduction but one of the principal themes, completely integrated with the rest of the structure; a first phrase that begins with the wrong harmony and moves to the tonic; an opening note that is finally understood as the last resolving harmony of the end of the exposition; an initial phrase that later becomes a modulation from the last cadence of the exposition back into the central tonality. No wonder Chopin is sometimes characterized as a composer uninterested in and uninspired by sonata form. The misprint is a sign that one of the original engravers and most of the succeeding editors had no idea what Chopin was up to, felt themselves at a loss with this structure. That was why they were not able to see the correct reading, which was in front of their eyes all the time. They could not even list it as a variant or acknowledge its existence.

You understand music, in short, when you think you do, when you feel comfortable with it. If you have heard it often enough, or even just seen it printed the same way many times, then it will sound and look right. Giving up a wrong reading or wrong style of performance can be as difficult as changing one's breakfast cereal or one's drinking habits, or the time one gets up in the morning. One of the greatest and most sensitive of Mozart conductors,

Fritz Busch, insisted all his life that singers execute the common cadence in recitatives without the appoggiatura that was absolutely traditional and universal during Mozart's lifetime.

The austere German tradition of playing Mozart exactly as it was notated was then in force (not really a worse tradition than the more fashionable one today of adding all possible excrescences to the music if they might have been executed during the composer's lifetime). Yet the unornamented written version is ugly by all of Mozart's standards of melodic shape, and the appoggiatura that makes it acceptable is strictly necessary, not merely desirable. Busch, however, was so used to the ugly version that the added grace note would have made him wince. Things too silly to be spoken, Beaumarchais remarked, can always be sung. We might add: nothing is too silly to be sung or played, once you get used to it.

I do not want to end on so pessimistic a note, because there is a series of more cheerful morals to be drawn. In the long run, wrong meanings are finally found out. Traditions of performance that no longer make sense are eventually changed—except perhaps in Vienna. Music creates meaning. New music creates new kinds of meaning.

2

HOW TO BECOME IMMORTAL

ON THE 12th of October 1770, in Rome, the brilliant English scholar and musician Charles Burney met an elderly Neapolitan composer of operas, Rinaldo di Capua. "He is not in great fashion now," remarked Burney, adding, "I found him in person not unlike Mr. Smith the English composer. He is very intelligent and reasonable in conversation." Burney reports part of their conversation, which has more than a little interest for us:

> He thinks composers have nothing to do now but to write themselves and others over again, and the only chance they have for obtaining the reputation of novelty and invention must arise either from the ignorance or want of memory in the public—as every thing both in melody and modulation that is worth doing has already been done over and over again. He confesses that tho' he has written full as much as his neighbours yet out of all his works perhaps not above *one* new melody can be found, and as to modulation it must be always the

same to be pleasing. What has not been done is only the refuse of thousands, who have tried and rejected it, either as impracticable or as displeasing. The only chance a man has for introducing new modulation in songs is in a short 2nd part in order to fright the hearer back to the first, to which it serves as a foil by making it comparatively beautiful.[6]

A responsive chord was awakened in Burney, as he goes on to remark: "We not only agreed in the above sentiments, but likewise about the noise and tumult of instruments in modern songs."

Those are quite proper conservative sentiments, still being expressed with heartfelt conviction today, and it is amusing to see how early postmodernism had its start. Thirty-five years later, however, Burney had understandably changed his mind about the state of music. He planned to publish his diaries, and wrote a comment in the margin next to this passage: "Let Haydn, Mozart and Beethoven answer this assertion."

We might reasonably agree that they have answered it. Burney wrote his marginal comment in 1805, when Beethoven was thirty-five years old; Rinaldo di Capua's mournful remarks had been made the year Beethoven was born. It is a pity that Charles Burney's famous daughter, Fanny, destroyed most of her father's exceedingly voluminous diaries (largely because his frankness and sharpness of speech threatened her almost pathological hankering after respectability). He was a perceptive and witty observer, in touch with most of the important musicians of his time, and we would have been able to follow the gradual changes in musical opinion and climate that had taken place between Burney's agreement with the old Neapolitan's sad philosophy of music history and the victorious establishment of the great triumvirate by 1805.

By this time Mozart had been dead for almost fourteen years and Haydn was too weak to compose. Beethoven was unchallenged throughout Europe as the greatest living composer of instrumental music. Even more, he was generally recognized as having surpassed his famous predecessors. This, of course, did not prevent critics from greeting each new work as a disappointment after his by then acceptable achievements of the previous years. When I was a small child, *The New York Times* received every new creation of Igor Stravinsky with hostility, but even then I knew, like everybody else, that he was the greatest living composer—and I knew it even without having heard much Stravinsky or even any of the more recent works at all. It is a mistake of music historians to rely too much on journalists and music critics to assess a composer's reputation, as we generally find a certain delay in their transmission of the more influential professional judgments. There is a revealing sardonic comment by Leopold Godowsky on a well-known statement of Paderewski, who once boasted, "When I don't practice for one day, my fingers know it; for two days, and my friends know it; for three days and the whole world knows it." Godowsky added: "On the fourth day, the critics hear about it." In any case, poets and novelists are generally better reporters of the general state of musical opinion than music journalists, who most often have an ax to grind, or, quite reasonably and justifiably, a more limited set of prejudices to broadcast.

In instrumental music Beethoven had no rival by 1805 after he had composed the *Eroica* Symphony. Opera was a different matter: here his only work had only a minor success, and he never acquired the prestige of Cherubini (whose seriousness he admired) or later of Rossini (of whom he was deeply jealous). The nature of his reputation is what concerns us here. He may have been misunderstood for much of his life—and we could make out a case for his being still misunderstood today—but his supremacy was acknowledged from a very early date. By 1801, for example, he was already considered the superior of Haydn as a composer of keyboard music, and his only real challengers in this field were Mozart (dead for almost ten years) and Clementi, who was becoming more famous as a publisher.* We should not be astonished by the early recognition: when Goethe was in his late twenties, critics were already talking about him in the same breath with Dante and Shakespeare, and he had to live for the rest of his life with that weight upon his character.

Musical reputations in the eighteenth and nineteenth centuries were most frequently characterized by comparisons with poets. Johann Ernst Wagner, a novelist admired and quoted by Robert Schumann (perhaps because he was a disciple of Schumann's beloved Jean Paul Richter), wrote in July 1807, in a review of Beethoven's *Eroica*:

> To grasp the different character of great composers sharply and profoundly and to represent them with discretion, this is—so long as music reels and staggers, dreaming, between Nature and Idea, and even, so to speak, between Appearance and Being—impossible. The only clear way once in a while to convey some small part of the character rests in the comparison of composers and poets.[7]

---

* See the brilliant series of articles in the *Allgemeine Musikalische Zeitung* of 1801 by Triest, summarizing the development of German music in the eighteenth century.

Wagner proceeds at once to his comparisons:

> If, for example, we therefore call Haydn the
> true Wieland of music, and compare the late
> Mozart with Schiller in many respects, or put
> some of van Beethoven's traits by the side of
> Jean Paul's, thus—and who can deny this?—
> a spark of light into the character of these com-
> posers is struck for us.[8]

There is unfortunately no "musical mirror" for
Goethe, he goes on to lament, but if only Anton
Eberl had not died so young, he would have provided
one. (Since Eberl lived to the age of forty, longer
than Mozart or Schubert, one would think he had
been given his chance.) This confirms the triumvirate—Haydn, Mozart, Beethoven—and almost
X, who did not quite make it, a pattern that would
continue and set the stage for Brahms's determi-
nation to become the X who was finally integrated
with the other three.

The coupling of Haydn and the witty rococo poet
Wieland had been made before, and it is evidently
the passionate and dramatic character of Schiller that
calls to mind the work of Mozart. The affinity of
Jean Paul with Beethoven is convincing enough:
Jean Paul was a difficult author, complex and exceedingly humorous, combining a learned style with

a strong popular bent in a mixture that makes few concessions to ease of reading. These observations of J. E. Wagner continue with an interesting comparison of Cherubini and the painter Jacques-Louis David (Cherubini's effects, like those of David, are too obviously calculated), and an explanation of why Mozart cannot fully provide a musical equivalent for Goethe, although both of them are *Mollists*, that is, basically composers in the minor mode. Wagner interestingly conflates the minor mode with the flat keys, or keys with flats in their signatures, mentioning "particularly F but also E flat." This has a real basis in late-eighteenth- and early-nineteenth-century practice and theory; the "flat" keys are related to the fundamental C major tonality by a subdominant character (believed to be less assertive, more feminine), just as C minor is characterized by a flat signature. What disqualifies "the great and wonderful Mozart" from being a convincing musical representative of Goethe, according to Wagner, is that he "lacked, not gaiety, but a good-humored humane cheerfulness." Like Goethe, however, Mozart is

unquestionably the most decisive of *Mollists*. Through the terror he inspires in the minor mode, through an overall rigorous system and a certain philosophical correctness, however,

Mozart remains most like Schiller, who even in the minor appears almost always as the strictist *Durist* [that is, a composer in the major, sharp, or dominant style].

This passage has the great merit of recognizing the *terribilità* of Mozart, all sense of which was soon to be lost and difficult to recover when he became a symbol of grace and a somewhat antiquated elegance. Wagner develops the idea rather fancifully by holding up Shakespeare as the author who combines major and minor most perfectly, "like the nightingale," and he claims that the composer who resembles him—rather than Laurence Sterne or Jean Paul Richter—will have finally earned the right to be called a musical humorist. He seems to be predicting Beethoven's eventual emergence in this role, for he calls him the sharpest *Durist*, but adds that in the *Eroica* the minor seems to be, "in secret," the reigning mode. In spite of his reserves about the symphony (in particular, Beethoven's insistent attempts to attack the rhythm of the bar line and to affirm it at the same time), there are moments when Wagner feels himself as if drawn into the "magical world of Shakespeare. And this arouses in us the most beautiful hopes for the future."

Most important for those of us today who want to assess the appreciation of Beethoven by his con-

temporaries is how Wagner treats the famous false
entrance of the horn just before the recapitulation:

> The transition to the first part [i.e., the re-
> transition]—in which the second horn timidly
> appears to try out or to *offer* the theme, at
> which point all the instruments, fortissimo and
> united in a monstrous trill, *quickly determine to
> take it up again*—this has hardly its equal in
> magnificence.

Finally, the coda receives extraordinary praise:

> The first apparent close, disturbed by a great
> and astonishing organ point, followed by the
> general filling out of the simple theme, broad-
> ening and swelling, until the most powerful
> heavenly sounding-together in the higher
> choir—all this, accomplished in a completely
> new kind of church style, throws open the doors
> of the heart with wondrous force, and fills us
> with unspeakable astonishment.[9]

These are interesting expressions from a critic who
began by saying, in the correct Romantic fashion,
that with work as experimental as Beethoven's ("who
fully merits the name of an aspiring spirit") only a

true description of what the listener hears or feels is possible, "as new, unknown seeds strewn in the field of time. —A judgment in the ordinary sense would be an extremely foolish beginning." When Wagner writes about "a completely new kind of church style," I am not sure if he intends to refer to the originality of Beethoven's counterpoint, or if he is impressed with the exalted, almost hymn-like quality of some of the passages in the coda.

The matching of composers to poets was by then a popular strategy. Wagner probably inherited the critical trope from Jean Paul's *Flegeljahre*, published in 1804–5, where an argument between German and Italian musicians is described:

> A dim spark of the war to come glowed during the dinner, with the simple remark by a German about the great German triad, when he said Haydn is the Aeschylus, Gluck the Sophocles, and Mozart the Euripides of music. Someone else said, it was all right about Gluck, but Mozart was the Shakespeare of music. The Italians joined in to flatter the conductor and said that in Naples they could show Mozart a thing or two.[10]

This appears to be a parody of a popular way of talking about music, and, in fact, we find the procedure already developed in the *Memoirs* of a minor composer, Karl Ditters von Dittersdorff, where he describes a conversation he had in the 1780s with Emperor Joseph II in which he distinguished Haydn and Mozart at the emperor's request by comparing Haydn to Wieland (a comparison retained, as we saw, by Wagner) and Mozart to the difficult philosophical poet Klopstock. The appearance of Shakespeare in Jean Paul's dialogue is a sign of the times; he was for almost all these critics a touchstone.

In his famous articles of 1811, the first real masterpieces of musical journalism, E.T.A. Hoffmann did not mention Shakespeare, but he gave a new and permanent cast to the perception of Beethoven, and it was one that depended on a radical reevaluation of Shakespeare criticism. There had never been any lack of admirers of Shakespeare after his death, but he was most often characterized either as a wild, untamed genius, a child of nature who refused to accept the rules of art and whose work suffered thereby, or sometimes simply as a genius whose art could afford to dispense with the rules. In either case, he was not a recommended model for a young and aspiring poet or playwright who wanted a successful career. With Friedrich Schlegel, and then later with his brother August Wilhelm, and finally with Coleridge, the literary personality of Shakespeare was given a strikingly new turn. Shakespeare, Friedrich Schlegel declared, was in reality the most "correct" of all poets, the ideal model: he

[47]

alone had been able to do away with the artificiality
of style and convention to create his own forms. He
now became the authority to imitate, although naturally his influence was in general disastrous (except
in the case of Heinrich von Kleist, who adopted
both a Shakespearian structure and a Shakespearian
prosody and succeeded magnificently with at least
two of his plays, *Penthesilea* and *Der Prinz von Hom-
burg*). When Hoffmann at the opening of his great
review of the Piano Trios opus 70 called Beethoven
the composer, denied that he was a wild, untamed
genius with an uncontrolled imagination, and described him instead as the "soberest" of all composers, "since everything he writes comes out of the
nature of sound," the implicit reference to Shakespeare was certain to be grasped by all of his readers.

If we compare Hoffmann's characterization of
Beethoven with Ludwig Tieck's dialogue on music
in *Phantasus*, published in 1812, we can see how far
in advance of his contemporaries Hoffmann was. Of
course, Hoffmann was a fine musician (if not a composer that has to be taken seriously, as some German
music historians would now like to persuade us) and
Tieck was only an amateur. Nevertheless, Tieck's
discussion registers a controversy about Beethoven
that shows both how badly and how well he was
understood, and it reveals important aspects of the
history of taste that bear directly on Beethoven's
work. Above all, we can see how closely knit the

European cultural community was, and how inter-dependent the aesthetics of literature and music.

The collection of stories and plays written over a fifteen-year period that Tieck put together in *Phantasus* is framed, as in Boccaccio's *Decameron*, by a conversation among cultivated men and women; the dialogue on music is central to Tieck's conception of literature and art in general.[11] Some of the discussion is representative of a movement that had begun some twenty years before with an attack on modern religious music, a rediscovery of Palestrina, and a claim that the ancient liturgical music that everyone thought had to be sung *a cappella* was the only style fit for the expression of religion. The chief composer active in this movement was Michael Haydn—not, in fact, a very impressive figure—and the new attitude to church music explains why Joseph Haydn once said that his brother's religious music was superior to his own. The fashion had its influence on the music of Joseph Haydn, however, and then on the work of Beethoven—at first in the most minimal way (his C Major Mass begins with only two notes sung *a cappella*).

The most extreme doctrine of this movement was the belief that only religious music—and only pure vocal religious music—was worthy of admiration. In Tieck's dialogue, a character called Ernst is the voice for this musical version of the Romantic religious revival:

Even earlier it had been a turning point in my life to become acquainted with this true old vocal music: I had always thirsted for the highest music and believe that I possessed no sense for this art before my sense and my hearing were awakened by becoming acquainted with Palestrina, Leo, Allegri, and those older figures who are now seldom or never mentioned by music lovers . . . Since then, I think I have come to understand that only this is the true music, and that the stream that was brought into the profane luxury of our operas only to be dammed up with wrath, revenge, and all the passions has become muddy and impure; for among the arts, music is the most religious—it is all piety, longing, humility, love. It cannot be pathetic, and to insist upon its strength or force, or to want it to exhaust itself in despair, is to make it lose its spirit, and it becomes only a weak mimic of speech and poetry. [12]

This is clearly not only anti-Beethoven but also anti-Mozart, and one of the other characters of the framing dialogue, Lothar, reminds Ernst of the time past when he used to adore Mozart. Ernst does not deny his former admiration, but "you must not ask me to listen to a requiem by him, or try to persuade me that he, or most of the moderns, could really have composed sacred music."[13] In *Phantasus*, the condemnation of modern liturgical music even extends to Haydn's *Creation*, and indeed the initial success of this work was considerably jeopardized by this musical equivalent of the Nazarene school of painting, the fashion for a dogmatic return to a supposed medieval purity. (Charles Burney's enthusiastic rediscovery of Josquin des Prés was fundamental in this movement.)

The eloquent praise of Mozart in this dialogue is colored by these modish opinions, but the ambiguity does justice to the power of his music. Ernst finishes by saying: "Heaven and hell, which had been separated by measureless gulfs, are magically and terrifyingly united in [his] art, which was originally pure light, quiet love, and religious praise. So Mozart's music appears to me." The defense of modern style that follows takes up the cause of instrumental music and leads, of course, immediately to Beethoven. The opposition of vocal and instrumental forms that appears so frequently at that time is similar to the arguments in the visual arts on the relative merits of color and line: "It was reserved for the most recent age, Lothar continued, to express the wonderful richness of human mind and sensibility in this art, especially in instrumental music."[14] It is clear that instrumental music was now considered the center of music, and the champions of vocal music were like the contemporary French advocates

of a restoration of the Bourbon line—nostalgic amateurs of an irrecoverable past.

For those who are interested in how the classical
canon was constituted, it should be pointed out that
only three modern composers are mentioned in
Tieck's dialogue: Haydn, Mozart, and Beethoven.
Even though Beethoven is introduced critically, he
is the only living composer who is given any consideration here. The presentation is controversial:

> As it always happens to human beings when
> they want to go beyond all limits and achieve
> the last and most sublime effects, passion shat-
> ters and splinters, becoming the opposite of its
> original greatness; so it happens to great talents
> in this art. If we may call Mozart mad, Bee-
> thoven often cannot be distinguished from a
> raving lunatic: he seldom follows through a
> musical idea or theme and is content with it,
> but leaps through the most violent transitions
> and, in his restless struggle, seeks to escape,
> as it were, from imagination itself.

This is, in fact, not entirely negative as a description
of Beethoven's music, although not very perceptive,
and we may take it as reflecting an important strand
of contemporary critical opinion. It calls forth an
immediate defense that brings the discussion to a

laconic close, and the banal style makes it more rather than less significant, as it implies that this conclusion was one generally acceptable to the cultivated German society represented by the dialogue:

All these new profound strivings, said Anton, are not foreign to my temperament. They sound like the rushing of the stream of life between stony banks, which tumbles musically over crags and confining rocks in a romantic wilderness. The only thing I don't understand is how Haydn's *Creation* and *Seasons* could give pleasure to almost everyone, although their childish painting defies all higher meaning. His symphonies and instrumental compositions are for the most part so splendid that one would never have believed he could go so far astray.[15]

The condemnation of the Haydn oratorios is a testimony to their continued popularity, in spite of their running contrary to fashionable aesthetic movements. The oratorios are, indeed, a summary of certain eighteenth-century ideals even if they were a new departure for Haydn.

Tieck's criticism of Beethoven needs comment: it was odd to reproach him, of all composers, with an inability to follow through a musical idea. To understand the attack, we need to look back to Dittersdorff's remarks about Mozart made thirty years before, which I have already mentioned:

> He is unquestionably one of the greatest original geniuses, and I have never yet known any composer who possesses such an astonishing wealth of themes. I wish he were not so extravagant with them: he doesn't let the listener catch his breath; just when one is about to reflect on a beautiful theme, another splendid one has already presented itself and drives out the earlier one, and it keeps going on like that until, in the end, one cannot retain any of these beauties in one's memory.[16]

The complaints about Beethoven in the *Phantasus* are identical to these reproaches leveled at Mozart in the 1780s, although expressed in somewhat stronger terms. It is a criticism more revealing about the critic who makes it than about the work in question, and it is more applicable to Mozart than to Beethoven. It is true that Mozart has "an astonishing wealth of themes"; Beethoven, by contrast, is often remarkable for his economy of themes, and, far from being unable to follow through a musical idea, he often seems unwilling to let one drop. It is interesting, nevertheless, that a reaction to such opposing kinds of difficulty or strangeness in new music should be formulated in similar and very traditional ways. The formulation may be almost totally inappropriate, but the oddness of the new work is equated automatically with any other oddness experienced in the recent past. (This would explain why Richard Wagner, for example, was later called a "realist"—for *Tannhäuser* of all operas!—and described by Fétis as "a musical Courbet.")

Tieck's view of Beethoven must have reflected a fairly common reaction to the music, and this popular view had almost certainly inspired the most cogent part of E.T.A. Hoffmann's essays, which had a profound influence on the foundation of music analysis: his description of the way not only a single movement but often an entire symphony or trio of Beethoven's seems to spring from a single theme or motif. This is a dramatic response to the contemporary point of view expressed by Tieck, and it finally became an essential element in the estimate of Beethoven that has continued to the present day: the conception of unity derived from a study of his works is at the origin of the development of musical style through the works of Schönberg and Boulez. Since Hoffmann, the belief that great works spring organically from a single tiny seed is so influential that we have tried to read Beethoven's method back into music of the past—sometimes, but not always, with great success—and we have even been embarrassed by the evident greatness of composers like

Verdi where this method does not work, or is insufficient. In this sense, the music of Beethoven is literally the origin of our conception of musical analysis, and this has unnaturally restricted analysis by limiting it almost entirely to methods of examination relevant to his music.

In sum, not only is the prestige of Beethoven firmly in place by 1811, but the critical methods of justifying that prestige have already been elaborated. Not enough attention, however, has been paid to Hoffmann's observation that the motivic relationships in Beethoven are difficult even for professional musicians to hear—unless, as he says, the two versions of a motif follow each other immediately or have the same bass (that is, have the same harmonies). From the beginning, we must realize, Beethoven's music demanded a kind of close listening, a kind of analytic attention, that had never been required in music before. I do not mean that the music of Bach, for example, does not repay the kind of close examination that we bring to bear so happily on Beethoven, but the details in Bach most interesting to the modern analyst are not capable of being set audibly in relief in performance without considerable distortion of the music. Analysis has a direct correspondence with execution: the music of Bach frequently demands dynamic articulation, but it is always an expressive articulation that is needed, not one that elucidates motivic structure. In Beethoven, too, of course, the dynamics very often have an expressive purpose, but they also serve to clarify: they emphasize the independence of the different motifs and bring out the way one theme is created from another. For example, the major and minor themes at the opening of the Sonata in A Major for Piano and Cello are illuminated by the dynamic accents in the minor theme, and their identity is confirmed:

The dynamics in Beethoven often function as essential motivic elements; the Piano, Crescendo, Sforzando, and Piano in the opening of the Sonata for Piano in E-flat Major, opus 31, no. 2, are all motivic as well as expressive:

With the exception of Burney, I have been bringing only the testimony of German witnesses to the
establishment of Beethoven's reputation—this is,
perhaps, only natural, not only because Germany
and Austria were the acknowledged centers of pure
instrumental music but also because of a growing
nationalistic pride in German culture. On Novem-
ber 3, 1812 (during the same period from which
we have been drawing so much of our evidence), the
poet Joseph von Eichendorff was lying ill and received a letter from an aristocratic friend, Otto
Heinrich, Graf von Loeben, expressing nothing but
extravagant admiration for the work of Ludwig
Tieck (I should not think it would help the con-
valescence of a sick poet to praise another poet to
him). An excerpt from this letter may shed further
light on the nature of Beethoven's prestige at this
time: "Who has given us back poetry [as Tieck has]
in *Zerbino, Oktavian, Genoveva*? I think I comprehend
Tieck in the deepest and most personal sense like
Albrecht Dürer, Beethoven, Novalis."[17] We can see
from this interesting triad that Beethoven had been
taken up by the radical young men of the German

Romantic movement. Except for the nationalistic flavor, this is very like the way the cause of Richard Wagner was taken up in France by avant-garde poets like Charles Baudelaire, Stéphane Mallarmé, and Catulle Mendès when he was being attacked by the members of the conservative Jockey Club. The presence of the Renaissance artist Albrecht Dürer alongside the two modern figures of Beethoven and the Romantic philosopher Novalis is only another proof of avant-garde ideology. Dürer had been, if not rediscovered (he had never completely disappeared from view), at least powerfully taken up by the Nazarene brotherhood, the young generation of painters intimately connected with the Jena circle, in which so much of early Romantic theory was given its most persuasive form. To this group belonged Friedrich Schlegel and his brother August Wilhelm, Novalis, Tieck, the theologian Friedrich Schleiermacher, and the young poet Clemens Brentano, who, with his friend Achim von Arnim, was to compile the famous collection of folk and pseudo-folk poetry *Des Knaben Wunderhorn*. The Nazarene painter Philipp Veit was Friedrich Schlegel's stepson, the child of Schlegel's wife, Dorothea Mendelssohn, by a previous husband. (It may help to understand the closely knit character of European culture at that time if one remembers that Felix Mendelssohn was Dorothea's nephew, and that he attended Hegel's lectures in Berlin.) One of the most

CHARLES ROSEN

impressive newspaper articles about Beethoven's genius written during his lifetime was by Clemens
Brentano.

Burney's marginal jotting about Haydn, Mozart,
and Beethoven, mentioned before, warns us not to
assume that the acknowledgment of Beethoven's
supremacy stopped at the German and Austrian
frontiers. An amusing witness to this comes to us
slightly later in the person of Charles Lamb, who
in 1821, six years before Beethoven's death, wrote
an essay against the appreciation of music entitled
"A Chapter on Ears." He has, he says, no ear for
music: ". . . *sentimentally* I am disposed to harmony.
But *organically* I am incapable of a tune." Operas
and oratorios are bad enough, he remarks, but even
worse are "those insufferable concertos, and pieces
of music, as they are called . . ." Listening to pure
instrumental music for Lamb ("empty instrumental
music," as he terms it) was like reading a book that
was all punctuation, or like gazing at empty frames
and trying to invent pictures. Worst of all was German instrumental music. Lamb had a friend who
would convert his drawing room into a chapel, and
play solemn anthems on the organ. But then

> this master of the spell, not content to have
> laid a soul prostrate, goes on, in his power, to
> inflict more bliss than lies in her capacity to
> receive,—impatient to overcome her "earthly"

with his "heavenly,"—still pouring in, for pro-
tracted hours, fresh waves and fresh from the
sea of sound, or from that inexhausted *German*
ocean, above which, in triumphant progress,
dolphin-seated, ride those Arions *Haydn* and
Mozart, with their attendant tritons, *Bach, Beethoven*, and a countless tribe, whom to attempt
to reckon up would but plunge me again into
the deeps,—I stagger under the weight of harmony, reeling to and fro at my wit's end . . .

We can see that by 1821, and probably much before,
Beethoven's fame is international, and that the trin-
ity remains fixed except that Johann Sebastian Bach
has now been added to the German canon. (Why is
Handel missing from the select group? Because, for
Lamb, Handel was an English composer.)

We must not imagine that prestige necessarily
implies frequency of performance. The fame of Mozart's *Marriage of Figaro*, for example, was international, but after its premiere in Vienna it was given
only a few performances, and it was then completely
dropped from the Viennese repertory for decades.
Too difficult to produce in Italy, and too long, the
original four acts of the opera were divided there
into two evenings, and for the last two acts Mozart's
music was thrown out and the libretto reset to music
by another composer. On the other hand, it was a
great success at Prague, where opera was not a court-

financed institution and a much more popular form
of support had to be elicited. Beethoven's fame was
uncontested around 1820, but his music was not,
in fact, played very often in Vienna at that time;
and it is significant that his friends complained that
no performances of symphonies by Mozart or Haydn
were to be heard either. Mozart, too, for a few years
toward the end of his life, just before *The Magic
Flute* gave him a real popular triumph, found it
difficult to attract audiences, although his importance and status were never in question. Similarly,
the prestige of Alban Berg's *Wozzeck* 150 years later
was very great among professional musicians for
many years before it was performed except on rare
occasions.

More important than frequency of performance,
if we wish to grasp how a composer was understood
by his contemporaries, is the nature of the milieu
in which his music was performed, the character of
the audience, and the program. In 1810, the composer Johann Friedrich Reichardt, who was also a
Berlin critic and the editor of the most influential
music magazine in Europe, traveled to Vienna and
wrote an account of his trip. He gave up some of
his beloved morning promenades in order to attend

the beautiful quartet concerts of Herr Kraft and
of Herr Schuppanzigh [more or less the official
Beethoven violinist], who have begun once

more a new subscription series. Just as in Kassel, where I made it my duty to be present at all the rehearsals of the Mozart operas, so that, at least on the part of the orchestra, they were played as well as possible, and I had the benefit of getting to learn the most wonderful masterpieces better and more completely than before, to fathom their greatest profundities and to follow their highest flights, so these quartet concerts offered me again the great profit of getting to know completely and thoroughly the new and most recent works in this form of Haydn, Mozart, and Beethoven—of which, since I gave up playing the violin, so much had escaped me. Through the recently established amateur quartet, I now still hope to have the joy of appreciating again these ever beloved works, some of the older Haydn quartets.[18]

Mostly quartets by Haydn, Mozart, and Beethoven were performed at each of Schuppanzigh's subscription concerts, although twice there was a quartet by Bernhard Romberg, a cellist who once, having played Beethoven's Quartet opus 59, no. 1, was so angered by the music that he tore his part from the stand, threw it on the ground, and stamped on it —proper and traditional behavior when faced with an unfamiliar masterpiece.

Several points of interest might be briefly signaled

CHARLES ROSEN

in Reichardt's account. The first is that the string quartet was not principally an amateur form but a public one played at concerts for which subscriptions were sold. Older works in this form, we see, might be performed by amateurs, but the newer works were presented by virtuoso professionals. Piano sonatas were considerably more private, and Beethoven's were almost never performed at public concerts in Vienna during his lifetime—this may seem paradoxical when we think of the clearly public *concertato* style of many of them, like the *Waldstein* Sonata, but public virtuosity in a private context must have made these works even more effective than they are today, played for a public of thousands.

It is significant, too, that Beethoven's quartets were almost invariably presented together with quartets by Haydn and Mozart, perhaps a means of affirming as well as acknowledging the tradition in which they were to be understood, to emphasize Beethoven's acceptance into the pantheon. Very curious is Reichardt's phrase on this matter, when he speaks of "the new and most recent works in this form of Haydn, Mozart, and Beethoven, of which . . . so much had escaped me." In 1810, Mozart had been dead for almost two decades and Haydn had composed no complete quartet since 1800, yet Reichardt applies the expression "new and most recent" not only to Beethoven's compositions. This suggests that the great string quartets of all three

[64]

composers, except for Haydn's earlier works, were not easy to hear in Berlin, which had a less active musical life than Vienna. It would seem that Reichardt knew in advance what he wanted to listen to, or what he felt that he ought to be listening to as soon as he had the chance.

We can see that canonic status is accorded to the works of a composer not by posterity, or at least not by a posterity as distant in time as is sometimes thought; nor does it depend very much on whether the works are frequently performed for the public in every important musical center. To a certain extent, canonic status is actually built into some new works, partly by the way they impose themselves on an already substantial musical tradition. This may explain why it is so difficult to alter a firmly installed canon in any radical way, or to dislodge works that have been an integral part of it for some time. I do not mean that it is not worthwhile to attempt a revision of the canon or that no success is possible. A few valuable minor changes have been made to our sense of the basic material of the history of music, and other alterations are still waiting to take hold. Gesualdo has not displaced Monteverdi or Palestrina but has won a permanent place; on the other hand, the attempt to convince us that Telemann is a major composer appears to have been abandoned. Alkan has not had the breakthrough his admirers had hoped for. Attacks on Tchaikovsky have not had much success in removing his music from the repertory; his credit with performers has not changed a bit. This is not really a question of personal taste: one may quite consciously prefer some trivial music to grand—Offenbach to Cherubini, say—without making much of a dent in one's own judgment of their relative merits; we have trouble enough revising our own standards of criticism without having to pretend to reform everyone else's. Any truly major revision of the basic canon would entail not simply a reevaluation of a number of neglected composers but a wholesale rejection of the entire Western musical tradition—this, of course, seems to many people today a commendable program, no matter how difficult to carry out.

It may not be strictly true to say that it was Beethoven himself and not posterity who decided that Beethoven was the culminating point of the classical tradition, but it would be at least as true as the fallacy that later generations alone determined his status, that the decision was a reasoned and voluntary one—and that it might have turned out otherwise. Events and Beethoven conspired to make it come out exactly the way it did. The pressure of a cultural elite ensured Beethoven's prestige, and he collaborated with it in order to guarantee the success of his reputation; perhaps collaboration does not exactly describe a strategy that depended on the continuous violation of the norms the elite wished to impose and on the production of works that shocked and astonished even more than they pleased, but provocation was already an acknowledged strategy in the development of style. Both Mozart and Haydn attained canonic status during their lifetimes, certainly by the 1780s, and part of their success was overcoming the resistance of both amateur and connoisseur, a resistance which, one may say, they helped to create as well as to vanquish. When Count Waldstein, Beethoven's patron, sent the twenty-one-year-old composer from Bonn to Vienna in 1792 with the words, "You are going to receive the spirit of Mozart from the hands of Haydn" (Mozart had recently died), the plan was already mapped out. Posterity had very little to say in the matter: it could have refused to confirm, but that would have meant in great part rejecting the Viennese and even the entire Central European musical traditions.

Of course, history may still have some surprises for us, and there will surely be revisions of the past. In his visit to Vienna, Charles Burney made the acquaintance of an eccentric Portuguese abbé:

> . . . a person of very singular character; a kind of Rousseau, but still more original . . . He is determined to be independent, and hates to be talked of by the world, and almost to talk to anyone in it . . . He plays very well on the

large Spanish guittar, though in a very peculiar style: with little melody, but, with respect to harmony and modulation, in the most pleasing and original manner . . .

This Abate is the extraordinary musician that I mentioned before, who, disdaining to follow in the steps of others, has struck out a new road, both as composer and performer, which it is wholly impossible to describe: all I can say of his productions is, that in them melody is less attended to than harmony and uncommon modulation; and that the time is always difficult to make out, from the great number of ligatures and fractions; however, his music, when well executed, which happens but seldom, has a very singular and pleasing effect: but it is certainly too much the work of art to afford great delight to any ears but those of the learned. [19]

None of the abate's guitar compositions have come down to us, so we cannot determine how eccentric they were. Would they sound banal to us if some of them turned up? Would they alter our view of music in Vienna during the 1770s? More to the purpose, should the existence of a composer of that kind, as Burney relates, lead us to alter, or at least inflect, our view of music in Vienna during that era?

Perhaps we may close with one more testimony to Beethoven's prestige in 1812, this one from the correspondence of Goethe and his friend the composer Karl Friedrich Zelter. Goethe writes on September 2 from Karlsbad:

> I learned to know Beethoven in Töpliz. His talent astonished me: but he is unfortunately a completely intractable personality, who is not wrong to find the world detestable, but that does not make it more agreeable for himself or for others. On the other hand, he is to be pardoned and very much to be pitied, since his hearing deserts him, which perhaps harms the musical part of his existence less than the social. Besides, his laconic nature will perhaps be doubled by this loss.

Zelter replied a few days later, on September 14:

> What you say about Bethofen [*sic*] is certainly true. I, too, regard him with terror. His own work seems to cause him secret horror: a feeling that is set aside far too frivolously in our recent culture. His works seem to me like children whose father is a woman or whose mother is a man. The last work of his that I encountered (*Christ on the Mount of Olives*) seems to me like an indecency whose basis and purpose are eter-

nal death. Music critics, who seem to understand everything better than naturalness and propriety, have poured out praise and blame about this composer in the strangest fashion. I know musical people who once found themselves alarmed, even indignant, on hearing his works and are now gripped by an enthusiasm for them like the partisans of Greek love. What a state one can get into over this can be imagined, and what can come out of it you have shown clearly enough in *The Elective Affinities*.[20]

No document gives a clearer or more striking idea of what it was like to experience the music of Beethoven during his lifetime. This mixture of perception, misunderstanding, ignorance, shock, and fascination is perhaps the greatest tribute written to his music. The view of Beethoven as a kind of sexual monstrosity is astonishing (and it also casts a very revealing and unsuspected light on what *The Elective Affinities* is about). If we are ever to comprehend what this music meant to those who heard it for the first time, the initial repulsion so explicitly expressed by Zelter must be taken into account.

I have never believed that the historian should seek to perpetuate the misapprehensions of the past, and it is true that we understand Beethoven today better than his contemporaries did, better, above all, than the generation that immediately followed him, including his own most important pupil, Karl Czerny. Nevertheless, there are aspects of the past that we must make a continual effort to recover. From 1812 until the present, the supremacy of Beethoven has never been seriously challenged, nor should it be. On the other hand, the initial resentment and even repulsion that this supremacy entailed did not completely vanish, and it clearly comes to the surface in composers as far apart as Chopin, Stravinsky, and Debussy. ("Now the development section is beginning, I can go out and smoke a cigarette," Debussy once remarked at the performance of a symphony by Beethoven.) If it was never made explicit by a later German composer, so far as I know, that is probably because it has been unconsciously suppressed for cultural and nationalistic reasons. Something of the same indignation, even repulsion, was excited by the music of Mozart, and that is even harder to reconstitute today. If we are, however, fully to understand the extraordinary achievement and power of these composers, it is an aspect that must be faced directly once again.

3

EXPLAINING THE OBVIOUS

MATHEMATICIANS TELL us that it is easy to invent mathematical theorems which are true, but that it is hard to find interesting ones. In analyzing music or writing its history, we meet the same difficulty, and it is compounded by another. For whom is it interesting? To paraphrase a famous remark of Barnett Newman, musicology is for musicians what ornithology is for the birds. We are faced with a puzzle at the outset. Is writing about music meant for the listener, and in what sense is it useful? One can see that program notes are beneficial when they deal with unfamiliar music, but largely in a negative sense—that is, it is helpful to warn the listeners that the piece they are about to hear will last not ten minutes but three-quarters of an hour; it keeps them from fidgeting nervously throughout the performance. (This is why, when playing Beethoven's *Diabelli* Variations, I always have the tempo marks of the thirty-three variations printed in the program, more as a map for the audience than for any other reason.)

Or is writing about music meant for the performer? I once played Beethoven's Sonata in A Major for Piano and Cello, opus 69, with Pierre Fournier, who always seemed to me the supreme model of elegance and sensitivity. Lewis Lockwood's study of the sketches and manuscript of this sonata had recently appeared, and I told Fournier that it was interesting to see that Beethoven had worked out on paper the derivation of the second theme from the first, literally by writing one directly underneath the other. (I have already mentioned this relationship in the second lecture.) Fournier was impressed, but remarked, "I have been playing this piece for fifty years, and I never noticed that they were really the same theme." Would his performance have improved if he had noticed it? I doubt it.

On the other hand, can we say that this analytical observation really referred to aspects of the music beyond Fournier's experience? Every performer of Beethoven has felt, through all the violent contrasts and disruptions of phrase and texture, a thread that binds the motifs together, that makes the second theme of opus 69 exactly right. Later—by Verdi when speaking about his own music—this unity would be called the *tinta*, the color or atmosphere that causes everything to blend into one whole. (For Verdi, the *tinta* is not realized primarily by motivic relationships, as in Beethoven, or even by a tightly symmetrical harmonic structure, as in Mozart, and that makes Verdi the despair of analysts for whom the concepts of motif and large harmonic areas are the only tools of dissection they have been trained to use.) The analyst's perception of the unity in Beethoven corresponded to Fournier's experience of the score of opus 69, and to his listeners' experience; everything in Fournier's performance brought this out, consciously or not. Hearing him play the sonata was as instructive as reading an analysis, and a good deal more enjoyable. Do we have to make explicit what we all take for granted?

The answer to this is "probably not," so long as we are dealing only with music of the specific and limited tradition in which we have been trained since childhood, and while that tradition is still an inspiration and has not yet become a dead weight. What happens, however, when we decide that our training has failed us? when we no longer take the style of playing in which we have been brought up for granted? when it finally occurs to us that it is absurd to play Bach, Mozart, Beethoven, Chopin, Brahms, Debussy, Prokofiev, and Boulez as they are taught in most conservatories, all with the same kind of warm vibrato on the violin? or, on the piano, the same monotonously "beautiful" tone production? the same kind of discreet pedaling? (even when, as in Haydn or Schumann, a distinct effect of blurring

on the instruments of their time was clearly intended), or the same kind of legato and articulation
of the phrase? (although Mozart's playing was called
"choppy" by Beethoven, and when Chopin was only
eighteen years old, critics commented that his playing hardly ever marked the beginning of the phrase
but sought an almost unbroken continuity). In our
time we can see an increasing dissatisfaction with
traditional ways of performing traditional music,
and it has become very up-to-date to develop new
ways of realizing scores, sometimes with the most
recent methods of reproducing sound combined with
archaeological studies of performance practice of the
past. We find a growing discontent with old ways
of conceiving the past, and some reckless experiments with performance in an attempt to find new
significance and meaning for the traditional reper-
toire.

Music has its existence on the borderline between
meaning and nonsense. That is why most attempts
to attribute a specific meaning to a piece of music
seem to be beside the point—even when the attri-
bution is authoritative, even when it is made by the
composer himself. In Schumann's *Carnaval*, it is
good to know that "Chiarina" is a portrait of the
young Clara Wieck, and it is not irrelevant to our
appreciation of the work, but it is oddly difficult to
define its pertinence to our understanding of the

music. What appears to be full enjoyment of the work does not depend on knowing the reference. Listening to pure instrumental music, as Charles Lamb observed, can seem like reading a book that is all punctuation. Music makes sense on its own, or we could not discover mistakes or discuss what seems to be wrong in performance or composition; nevertheless, it threatens to spill over easily into nonsense, or we could never be so puzzled to explain just what it means, or become so comfortable with faulty texts and traditions of performance that are demonstrably and logically wrong. All forms of culture, of course, can turn into nonsense or become meaningless acts carried out almost mechanically, but few arrive at the intense inane so easily as music, except for certain rituals at banquets and church services that continue to be performed unthinkingly when we have forgotten what they once meant. That is why it would seem so peculiar or even irrelevant to demand that music be reasonable or rational. No one would say that he wants to hear a "reasonable" symphony or listen to a "rational" performance of a Beethoven sonata—although, in reality, rules of logical coherence apply in both cases, or we could never detect misprints in a score or object to the lack of authenticity in an interpretation. Moments of crisis are precipitated, in fact, when the logic and the coherence disappear, when the tradition of performance itself seems to have lost its reason for existing. A sense of crisis periodically justifies our attempts to reinvent the practice of music, to discover new styles of interpretation and carry out experiments compounded equally of despair and of imagination.

The most regrettable aspect of these fashionable changes in performance style is that they almost always take place on the basis of sonority alone, not of meaning. Some years ago, for example, a few adventurous musicians took it into their heads to see what the combination of harpsichord and orchestral sound would be like—a very agreeable noise, in fact—and we suddenly heard the harpsichord placed close to the microphone on recordings of Haydn symphonies, destroying the wonderfully lean character of Haydn's occasional passages of two-part counterpoint with absolutely no warrant from the performance practice of Haydn's time. We know that Haydn and other musicians directed an orchestra from a keyboard, but has no one ever asked how much of the time the keyboard instrument was actually played, or how audible it was when it was played—and audible to whom? Could the public hear it, or only the musicians of the orchestra? For some years, hairpin dynamics —— ——— were scattered with profusion over Baroque music, often for no musical reason other than that it was believed to have been customary in the eighteenth century. I have witnessed—but not heard—*The Well-Tempered Keyboard* performed on the clavichord in a hall seating twelve hundred people, although the ear can only faintly pick up the sounds of this instrument in a small concert hall or good-sized living room. All these caprices indicated a profound and justifiable dissatisfaction with the current way of making music, and yet they have all mostly been dropped. This would tend to show that the effect of musicology on performance is often to inspire the more ambitious musicians to make a nuisance of themselves. I sometimes long for the days gone by when performers were supposed to be ignorant, unthinking animals like tenors—or, better, like Plato's poets, who, as Socrates maintained, produce their works through inspiration and understand neither how they are created nor what they mean.

Intelligence is sometimes considered a handicap for a performing musician. Too much reflection, it is felt, will take the edge off the spontaneity that is necessary for a performance to carry conviction. It is granted that a pianist must have a certain instinctive intelligence, the kind that owls have, for example, which enables them to catch mice. This is the primitive mental activity that allows pianists to hit the right notes without thinking and remember when to come in at the end of the ritornello in a concerto. Discursive thought might adulterate the emotional response that must be communicated to the listener.

It requires, however, at least some kind of low-grade cunning just to find the apt and proper emotional response. An aggressive interviewer on the French radio once asked me if I did not feel that my work as a pianist suffered from the fact that I reflected too much about the music I performed. I did not think of anything clever to reply until I had left the studio. I might have responded, with Diderot, that it is not the performer overwhelmed by his own passion who is the most effective; it is the musician who only appears to be spontaneously moved by the music but who is able to manipulate his own feelings in order to stir the emotions of the public. Any pianist who has toured with an orchestra and played the same concerto a dozen times in two weeks will understand the importance of simulating an emotion, of being able to call it up at will.

It is certainly true that knowledge leads as often to ineffective and misjudged performances as to good ones. It is sometimes claimed, however, that performances that are informed by knowledge and understanding are on a different level from the unthinking, instinctive ones, either higher or more profound, depending on which way you want to go. I am not sure this is correct, and the truth may lie, not in denying the proposition, but in reversing its direction. It may be that those musicians whose sense of their art is already reflective may be impelled to justify their temperament and inclinations *ex post facto*.

There used to be a union rule for the technicians who ran the tape machines at recording sessions, and took directions from the sound engineers and producers, that they be unable to read music—on the only too comprehensible grounds that if they could, it would give them an unfair advantage over their fellow technicians. There was, in fact, a technician at CBS Records who knew how to read a score but was forced to pretend ignorance: if you asked him to cut the tape, you had to give him a signal, and were not permitted to show him the score, indicating the place to cut by pointing at the text, if there was anyone else in the room.

It might sometimes appear as if performers were being enjoined by some kind of union regulation from using their common sense. I have heard as fine a pianist as Alicia de Larrocha play the last concerto of Mozart with the well-known misprint that makes a passage of the slow movement sound like Puccini's *Tosca*:

All those parallel fifths and octaves reminiscent of "Vissi d'arte" may sound very nice to us today, but they are not Mozart. What happened is that Mozart decided to double the melody in the piano with the flute, and then, in a wonderful last-minute inspiration, decided to double the flute as well with the violin an octave lower (a solo violin, of course, although most conductors persist in using six or more violins in spite of Mozart's writing "Solo" in the score). Adding the exquisite sonority of the flute with the violin an octave lower now produced parallel fifths and octaves with the music played by the left hand of the pianist. This was, of course, unacceptable to Mozart, who directed the pianist to transpose the left hand down an octave (he actually crossed out the notes in the score and wrote "Basso" over them), so reestablishing the correct voice leading and avoiding a harmonic effect that he would have found ludicrous. The original engraver of the first edition overlooked Mozart's direction, and editors, with some honorable exceptions, have been printing the Puccini-like passage ever since; many pianists continue to play it, savoring the sudden modern effect that this brings. (The *Neue Mozart Ausgabe* volume published in 1960 has the correct reading.)

A similar oversight occurs in the slow movement of Mozart's Piano Concerto in C Minor, K. 491, where Mozart added some beautiful accompanying wind parts with new harmonies to a solo piano phrase, and forgot to change the harmonies in the piano—this time with horrible effect, rather than a merely picturesque one. In this case, the *Neue Mozart Ausgabe* is as foolish as any other edition:

Even the editor of the well-known Eulenburg scores, Friedrich Blume, failed to notice the cacophony, and he has been emulated by many performers who no doubt imagine that if Mozart forgot to correct it, then it must be right.

Performers do not need to rely on misprints or slips of the pen to produce nonsense. One afternoon in a piano competition for which I unwisely agreed to be a member of the jury, I was surprised to hear three young pianists from Juilliard all play the transition linking the Maestoso to the Allegro of the first movement of Beethoven's Sonata in C Minor, opus 111; all three started the trill very slowly and suddenly doubled its tempo without warning. Since the trill begins in the Maestoso as thirty-second notes and continues unbroken into the Allegro as sixteenth notes, one would imagine that no intellectual effort would be required to conclude that the Allegro is exactly twice as fast as the Maestoso, that the trill should be played at a uniform speed throughout, and that the transition should not sound as if one had just shifted from first into fourth gear:

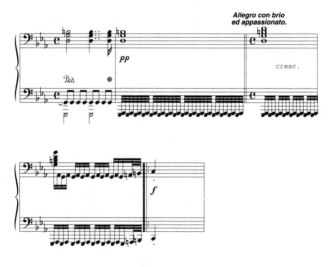

Most pianists, including myself, have wanted to play the Maestoso too slowly, as an Adagio (I have only recently come around to Beethoven's way of thinking), but even if we play the wrong tempo, those of us who had the good fortune to escape Juilliard when young at least have enough sense to accelerate the trill gradually and preserve the continuity conceived by Beethoven.

We may think it a pity that the distinction between musicology and performance is often made to sound like an opposition between thought and action. But it would be only fair, after my preceding mean-spirited attack on performers, to point out that intelligence is not, in fact, a prerequisite for success in musicology, either, although it has never been openly held to be a disadvantage. A pair of examples from two grand figures of the past may illustrate this. In Paul Henry Lang's once famous *Music in Western Civilization*, we find the following surrealist sentence, which was pointed out to me many years ago by Oliver Strunk: "Tchaikovsky does not belong in the company of the great in music; to call him the 'modern Russian Beethoven' is footless, Beethoven being patently neither modern nor Russian . . ." Strunk assumed that this Alice-in-Wonderland logic must be a misprint, but when he called it to Lang's attention, Lang was adamant. "It's what I wrote," he claimed stoutly, and stood by it.

Perhaps, after all, it is possible to reconstruct the way this inexplicable sentence came about. Someone in Lang's hearing must have made a clever joke: "to call Tchaikovsky 'the modern Russian Beethoven' is foolish, as *Tchaikovsky* was neither modern nor Russian"—and this was a witty device for pointing to Tchaikovsky's deep reliance on the German and French traditions, the strong international character of his music when compared with a fellow country-man like Mussorgsky. Lang misunderstood the joke, but appreciated its success and used it unthinkingly, preoccupied as he was with launching a virulent attack on Tchaikovsky, whom he judged, as he judged everything, from a parochial Central European perspective.

The second example comes from an even more distinguished figure, the most powerful German musicologist of the 1940s and 1950s, Friedrich Blume. In introducing his edition of Mozart's Concerto for Piano in G Major, K. 453, he describes the slow movement as being in "modified variation form." From the expression "modified" (whatever that may mean here), we can see that Blume uneasily realized that something was wrong, but even so, there cannot be a worse mistake in the description of form, since the slow movement of this concerto is in unproblematic sonata form, exemplifying even the most academic nineteenth-century versions of that pattern, and this is the polar opposite of var-iation form. (Sonata form assumes a series of structural transformations of harmony and melody, with new material added to old, and the old material restructured, not merely repeated and varied; variation form in Mozart, on the contrary, depends on an unchanging underlying structure, in which a single melody is repeated with changing ornamentation and texture.) The mistake is so foolish, in fact, that when I read it, I immediately assumed that there was a misprint, as the *last* movement of the concerto is indeed in *strict* variation form. Not so, however, as Blume eventually comes to grips with the last movement and describes it as in "rondo form with variations"; the only way in this case that one can arrive at rondo form (the alternation of two or more themes) is to be unable to identify the theme in one out of every two variations.

I offer these examples, not just out of malice, but to demonstrate that different kinds of intelligence are required for different kinds of musicology. While Blume had the managerial efficiency to organize a great musical dictionary like *Musik in Geschichte und Gegenwart* with enviable success, we need not pay any attention to what he had to say about musical form. There is no use holding a man responsible for what he cannot do, and there are as many different kinds of musicology as there are temperaments. Not everyone can decipher Beethoven's handwriting, recognize the watermarks in Mozart's

manuscripts, teach harmony, draw a Schenkerian
graph of a Haydn sonata, realize a figured bass in
Handel, fill out the proper accidentals in a fifteenth-
century mass, uncover the serial technique in a piece
by Pierre Boulez, give a lecture on classical Greek
music, or recognize the structural patterns in a Mozart concerto. We must assume, since we have no
reason to think otherwise, that Blume enjoyed the
Mozart Concerto in G Major as well as the next
man, even if he could not identify the form or even,
at times, recognize the main theme.

There are two basic ways of writing about Western music: analysis and historical interpretation; dis-
cussions of performance practice may be said to fall
between these two stools. Historical interpretation
is the grander task: assessing the significance, biographical, social, or cultural, of a work or a style in
terms of the composer's period or for the succeeding
generations allows the critic's imagination full play.
It is sometimes felt that cultural history is only a
disguised form of fiction. It cannot, however, be
done away with, and no attempt to write about
music can avoid practicing it. Even an aesthetic that
proclaims the autonomy of works of art will not
release music from history, as that aesthetic is itself
a historical assumption, basic to late-eighteenth-
century philosophy, above all that of Immanuel
Kant. Fortunately or unfortunately, it applies more

convincingly to music than to any other art, so well, in fact, that the belief that quartets and symphonies of Mozart and Beethoven rise above history can never be completely erased—the autonomy was written into them, so to speak; we are expected to listen to them as if they had no message and no social function, no other reason for existing than to be perceived. The autonomy of these works cannot be simply denied, even if it is transcended.

The difficulty of attaching a cultural or historical interpretation to music is evident; even the most interesting tends to seem arbitrary, as if the critic who advances it were merely employing an easy process of free association. You see this at once with biographical criticism, the most primitive form of historical interpretation. The simplest assumption is that an interesting work by the composer reflects some interesting aspect of his life. This assumption is plausible and not always unjustified. It works most effectively with a work of music that is melancholy, dramatic, or tragic; we need only look for something unfortunate that happened to the composer at the time of writing—generally easy to find, as most composers are either in debt or ill, or else crossed in love, unappreciated, and friendless. No life is free of adversity.

Biographical criticism, therefore, seems fairly safe, but it has its dangers. In *The Sonata in the*

Classical Era, William S. Newman quotes a German musicologist, Hanns Dennerlein, on Mozart's great dramatic Sonata for Piano in A Minor K. 310:

> Joining those who regard much of Mozart's music . . . as an expression of immediate personal experience, Dennerlein believes this strangely sad, quasi-Schubertian sonata was written while Mozart was still "dreadfully sad and depressed," with periodic "fits of melancholy," after his mother's death in Paris (July 3, 1778) and while he was trying desperately to get control of himself again.

This seems unexceptionable, but biographical interpretation is a slippery slope, and Dennerlein comes to the next sonata, the one in A Major K. 331, with the finale *Alla Turca*: "Dennerlein suggests that in another sense this work was also a counterpart of the preceding sonata. That is, having given vent to his grief in the other, Mozart now took this tender, loving means of honoring the memory of his departed mother." I presume Dennerlein was in earnest, but I hope that Newman copied this passage with a skeptical appreciation of the comedy of a composer's honoring his recently departed mother with a Turkish rondo. Unfortunately, the English scholar Alan Tyson has considerably disturbed the once accepted chronology of these Mozart sonatas, and their contiguity is no longer accepted.

Analysis is often thought to be the most objective of the various disciplines of criticism, as it is supposed simply to state what goes on in a piece of music; indeed, one occasionally hears claims made for analysis that would elevate it into a science. It has been attacked for that very objective stance and even been labeled "phallocentric"—or, more wittily, phallological—for its supposed efforts to dispense with subjectivity, considered a feminine trait. Analysis is anything but objective, however, and, as practiced today, imposes a very limited and constraining system of values on both composer and listener. The principal forms of musical analysis most popular today are motivic and harmonic: analysis of the motivic structure assumes that it is desirable for themes to be closely related in their pitch content; harmonic analysis postulates that a unified and centralized large-scale harmonic structure is a proof of competence and compositional superiority. Any work that does not stand up to these requirements is therefore defective.

Motivic analysis—the demonstration that two different passages are constructed with the same motif or similar ones—derives, as I observed the other day, directly from the practice of Beethoven, although the technique of motivic development can be traced back at least to the music of the fifteenth century. It is only too easy to produce uninteresting triviality by finding similar or identical motifs in unrelated passages, particularly in tonal music, as I shall hasten to explain; the final step toward nonsense is taken by attaching significance, and sometimes even a very specific referential meaning, to largely unrelated recurrences. There is, of course, nothing insignificant in Nature, God attends the fall of every sparrow, and meaning of some sort can be drawn from the discovery of any invariance. What kind of meaning is a different matter.

There are twelve notes to the chromatic scale, and the permutation of twelve objects can produce a very large number of patterns. In tonal music of the eighteenth century and most of the nineteenth, however, almost every theme outlines or implies the central tonic triad, and there are only three notes in a triad:

The permutation of three notes gives us only six possible arrangements, so the number of melodies whose underlying skeletons will resemble each other is ridiculously large. (That is why the Italian opera composer Rinaldo di Capua remarked in 1770 that no more original melodies were left; they had all been written already.) If, for example, the last movement of Mozart's Sonata for Piano in A Minor, K. 310, were to be scored and played as the finale of Schumann's piano concerto, we would remark admiringly on the way the composer has reconceived the theme of the first movement as the opening of the finale (and perhaps marvel at the way Mozart could prefigure the coding of Clara's name in the melody, since the first, third, and fifth notes are respectively C, A, and A):

I should like to demonstrate just how quickly one can come up with superficial and meaningless motivic relationships. Let us take one of the simplest of all motifs, three stepwise notes in a rising third, from the beginning of Beethoven's Quartet in

F Major, opus 135, a motif so common that it can be found in almost every piece of music ever written:

Beethoven characterizes this motif so strongly by its rhythmic texture that it would be humanly impossible not to notice that he almost immediately repeats it at the end of the second bar, but analysis does not exist to tell us anything as simple as that. We must seek out a rising third for which the relation to the opening will be more subtle, more sophisticated, harder to perceive. We find what we need at once in the sixth bar, first in the violins and then repeated at once in viola and cello:

This is not a very convincing example of a relation or an invariance with the opening motif, but they are heard closely enough together that you might be able to persuade a docile auditor that this is the way to listen to Beethoven. We must go further afield for an even less convincing and more obviously trivial example. There is one to our purpose a few pages on in the development section, where the three-note pattern both rises and then is inverted as a descent:

We now have three instances of one of the most common motifs in all Western music, a mounting three-note pattern which, I repeat, may be found anywhere you look for it, in whatever piece by whatever composer. This shows how easy motivic analysis can be. It may be taught in five minutes to any student, and he can produce term papers on motivic analysis while watching television or doing anything else that engages his mind while leaving his hands free.

I have, I am not ashamed to say, been cheating. I have not played the bars preceding the third occurrence of the motif in the development section:

The third appearance of the motif is, as you see, prepared by a repeated playing of the second one. If you cannot remember where the second example was first played and connect it up to the third, you cannot be said to be hearing the Beethoven quartet in any sense of that word that implies understanding.

I have further cheated by having omitted the cello and viola parts in the third example:

[95]

Here is the initial appearance of the motif, now played syncopated in the cello and viola, on the weak beats with the same pitches as the simultaneous motif in the violin but transposed down several octaves. Beethoven wants us to hear these relationships and sets them out for us. We can therefore link the first appearance with the other two; or rather—and I wish to emphasize this very strongly—Beethoven has linked up these motifs for us and has forced us to perceive both the invariance and the way the simplest possible succession of notes is both transformed throughout the piece and identified each time in its original form.

In short, what is interesting is not the identity of two motifs—that can be found anywhere in tonal music, as I have said—but the way that we are forced to perceive the transformation and the underlying invariance. That is why I claimed yesterday that Beethoven's music demanded an attentive kind of listening that had always been possible before but had never been so aggressively thrust upon the audience, with the exception of the more ambitious works of Joseph Haydn—and the demands are rarely as complex in Haydn, if they are often equally relentless.

The question omitted from so much analysis is: What has the composer done to make us responsible for hearing these relationships? And if these motivic relationships are not consciously perceived, then the question becomes: How else do these invariances enter into the experience of the work? Do they affect our sense of its character, determine its harmony, contribute to what has been called its "color"? If none of these questions can be answered, that does not necessarily mean that the motivic relationships, identities, or recurring patterns that we have analyzed have no interest, but the significance of the relationships discovered must be displaced from the work itself over to the musical language or to the psychology of the composer. They can no longer be considered as directly contributing to an understanding of the specific work of music.

Analysis explains the obvious, then; it tells us what we have known all along. It sets into relief the musical relationships that we have always somehow heard. Those that no one has experienced even unconsciously or subliminally before the critic has discovered them and pointed them out are necessarily less important than the ones that have been an essential part of the effectiveness of the musical work throughout its history. The most cogent analysis deals less with the esoteric than with the commonplace. It helps us to find out what we have not yet realized that we knew, brings to the surface that part of the experience of listening of which we were only partially aware. We ought to be suspicious of the critic who claims to hear what no one else has heard, finds significances invisible or inaudible to less perceptive eyes and ears. It is true, though, that becoming aware of what we have always known changes the nature of our knowledge in strange and unpredictable ways, and it clearly changes the way we listen to music. Aspects of the music that had previously acted upon us only indirectly take on a new clarity. The thematic relationships that Beethoven forced his contemporaries to take note of in his works may also be found in Mozart, and it is evident that Beethoven transformed the way one listens to Mozart. Today we emphasize certain aspects of Mozart's craft that must have affected his contemporaries more obscurely—more tactfully, we might say.

One of the constraints of motivic analysis is that it deals almost entirely with relationships based on rhythm and pitch. Certain musical patterns may, however, resemble each other by contour or profile alone, the pitches or intervals having been changed and the rhythms significantly altered. An interesting example of this kind of relationship comes from the same Beethoven quartet, opus 135. A short time after the beginning, a new theme appears in a simple, even rhythm:

This may be related in a naïve way to the opening motif:

Both motifs first go down, then up, and then down once more, although the second downward leap is smaller than the first. We might say that at this price we could demonstrate the motivic identity of any part of a piece with any other—down-up-down is not a pattern that would be hard to dig out of almost any page of music. Once again, however, it is Beethoven who forces the hidden identity upon our notice by playing the two forms together:

The first form is quirky, characteristic, and scherzando; the second is flattened out, mysterious, lyrical, and expressive. They set each other off, and perceiving an identical formal source is a pleasure at once intellectual and physical. The combination of the two forms embodies both a paradox and its witty resolution.*

All these various techniques by which Beethoven developed and transformed his motifs and his themes, added to the techniques of fragmentation and acceleration of the rhythmic structure of a single motif that he inherited from Haydn and Mozart,

---

* Elliott Carter pointed out to me that Roger Sessions paid particular attention to questions of contour and profile, even at the expense of blurring the identity of his motifs in terms of pitch and rhythm. Perhaps this weakening of a major aspect of his motifs contributed to the difficulty of Sessions's music.

make an almost metaphysical point about the nature of a work of music. It seemed to Beethoven's contemporaries, as E.T.A. Hoffmann observed, that very often at the basis of a long movement, or even a composition in several movements, there was a single, clearly defined source, a tiny musical molecule out of which the larger structure was derived. It is true that the initial inspiration of a Bach fugue is the theme, of which the contrapuntal possibilities of development, of stretto, could be perceived instantly by the composer, even before he began the actual composition of the fugue. Bach's students testified to his ability to calculate the contrapuntal possibilities of a theme at first hearing. In a work by Beethoven, however, this is not the way the central nucleus acts: what might be developed out of the short motif was essentially unpredictable. I am here begging the question whether the short motif is actually the inspiration of the work, or whether the original conception is a much larger idea; in any case, the significant building blocks of one of Beethoven's works are generally short, and —what is most striking—they seem to have a life of their own. The absolutely clear definition of the underlying motif from which everything will arise gives the appearance of rigorous logic to the structure that develops. The separate existence of the central motif is gradually confirmed by the entire

[101]

An die Musik

piece, and, like the rising third in opus 135, becomes clearer and more substantial as the work moves forward. The basic motif appears to be an ideal reality almost independent of all its different realizations in sound.

Although Schubert took so much from Beethoven and depended so heavily on his forms and his style, the ideal existence of this central motif no longer elicits the faith of composer or listener. Naturally, many of his works continue Beethoven's commitments to the hard-edged definition, but they are not always the finest or the most interesting. In some of his most extraordinary songs and chamber music, Schubert offers something much more fluid and indefinite for the motif. It is no longer a clearly defined ideal object appearing through different transformations but a simple interval that changes its identity as the music proceeds, expanding to encompass a larger range with a continuously more intense expressive charge.

As a demonstration—perhaps intended as one, given its title—we may take "An die Musik" ("To Music"). In this song, Schubert does not entirely abandon Beethoven's motivic substratum, but we can see him moving away from it. The opening vocal phrase is based on two falling sixths—D to F-sharp, and B to D—followed by a turn that is both ornamental and expressive:

This model four-bar phrase is succeeded by three bars, but it is really two overlapping four-bar phrases, as the left hand of the pianist has already begun the melody again, and the voice picks it up at the beginning of the next bar:

The second phrase is essentially a repetition of the first (if we count the bass of the piano as the opening of the phrase), but the second falling sixth (B to D) has now been enlarged to become a more dissonant and more expressive seventh (B to C-sharp resolved to the D).

In the following phrase the first falling sixth (D to F-sharp) is also enlarged into a more expressive seventh (E to F-sharp), and then rises even higher to an octave—"you have fired my heart with a warm love"—while still emphasizing the interval of a seventh (E down to F-sharp) on the descent that succeeds:

The interval, widened from a seventh to an octave with the ascent to the upper F-sharp (a rising sixth, in fact, from A to F-sharp), is repeated with the rhythm augmented—"you have sent me into a better world"—and the climax on the upper note is intensified:

Finally the two falling sixths of the singer's first phrase are recapitulated in the last phrase, first D to F-sharp, and then finally an A to C-sharp, which brings the resolution of a dominant harmony in place of the original B to D:

We could consider the initial falling sixth as a motif, but it would be more accurate to describe it as an expanding contour, each successive expansion more expressive than the last. The climax of the last phrase echoes the expressive turn at the end of the first phrase:

but it works less as a motif recalled than as a more vibrant version of the pitches transposed up an octave. The emotional power of the song does not depend on a treatment of motif but on a gradual and subtle expansion of the initial vocal space downward from sixths to sevenths and then upward to an octave.

In this great tribute to music, everything springs from the opening phrase, and in that sense Schubert is still working with Beethoven's aesthetic. The way it develops, however, is fundamentally opposed to Beethoven's method. Schubert does not use his opening motifs—the two falling sixths and the succeeding turn—for the energy buried within them. He uses instead the space that they have defined, stretching it, and achieves a short work in which every phrase is successively more expressive and more expansive than the preceding one. There is no pause in this development, no phrase before the postlude in which the tension is briefly relaxed in order to gather force again—and this tightness of organization is essential to the effectiveness of so short a song.

The lieder on poems by Friedrich Rückert display Schubert's most personal invention in its most concentrated form. "Du bist die Ruh" has a technique at once simpler and more powerful than "An die Musik." We start with the interval of a fourth, the

Du bist die Ruh

mein Aug' und Herz.

Kehr' ein bei mir, und schlie _ sse du still hin _ ter
dir die Pfor _ ten zu. Treib' an _ dern Schmerz aus die _ ser
Brust! Voll sei dies Herz von dei _ ner Lust, von dei _ ner
Lust.

diatonic notes within this interval arranged as a
motif and performed twice:

> *Thou art tranquillity, gentle peace,*
> *Yearning, and what stills it . . .*

With the next line:

> *I dedicate to thee, full of desire and sorrow*

the interval is expanded by a half step to an augmented fourth, and the inner notes are rearranged
to form an entirely different melodic shape. It is the
reappearance of the original elements in a different
order that makes this phrase so idiosyncratic and so
novel. The permutation of the four notes of the
original phrase (B-flat, C, D, and E-flat) transforms
the nature of the phrase by undercutting the identity
of the motif and placing the emphasis instead on
the interval defined by the four notes, now enlarged
by the addition of the A-natural. This seems to start
again, but once again expands the interval from a
diminished fifth to a perfect fifth and then to a sixth:

For a dwelling here my eye and heart

and then rounds off the melody with a symmetrical echo of the last two bars, now transposed to produce a tonic cadence, while the space defined by the melody of the whole first stanza is the basic tonic octave, from E-flat to E-flat:

The end of the second phrase may be heard as an inversion of the opening of the first, as the harmony implied in both cases has a characteristic and individual sound:

Nevertheless, the melodic progress is more clearly shaped by the widening of the space down to A-natural and then to A-flat in what follows.

Moving from a perfect fourth through an augmented fourth, a fifth, and a sixth, to the simplicity of the tonic octave gives a beautiful sense of purity and closure to the melodic space:

[111]

But after the pattern is repeated in the second stanza, the third opens up the form. Here Schubert further develops this technique of expanding the vocal space in the simplest and most astonishing fashion, starting with a chromatic alteration of the diatonic notes within the original interval of a fourth:

This eye-vault by your radiance alone illumined

The melodic line steadily rises, and goes one half step beyond what we are led to expect—in fact, what we are led to expect again each time we hear it, as the brilliance of the final A-flat that appears with the image of light always comes as a surprise, largely because the chromatic alterations seem at first to be resolved and canceled by the G-natural, giving it the air of a point of rest unexpectedly harmonized by a dissonance, a dominant seventh chord that demands the harmony of A-flat. Then the song is rounded off with a return to the end of the first stanza. It is the marked simplicity of the texture

[112]

that invests the slightest detail with such weight, and makes the reordering of the same notes so telling.

The basis of the technique is the exploitation of the singer's register. Starting with a very small part of the register, the expansion is downward at first, and then upward. The procedure reveals a profound understanding of how the human voice works, and how it can be used with the greatest economy to the greatest advantage. Expansion of the register is an effort for a singer, and this effort can be exploited for expressive effect. The essential elements of the melody are less the individual motifs than the simple stepwise expansive movement. The motivic patterns count for something, of course, particularly the opening and the final bars of each stanza, but they play a secondary role to the gradual widening of the initial interval described by the contour of the melody of the first two bars.

Another Rückert song, "Dass sie hier gewesen" ("That she was here"), reveals the same procedure with much greater richness. The ambiguity of the poem called up Schubert's most magnificent display of shaded contrasts, nuanced opposition, and synthesis. This is a foreshadowing of later Symbolist work, a poetry of empty rooms and the suggestion of presence by odors and the traces of tears left behind, and only the hint of a possible narrative behind the images in the poem. The first two stanzas give us:

> *That the east wind perfumes*
> *Breathes in the airs*
> *In this way he informs us*
> *That you were here*
>
> *That here tears flow*
> *In this way will you be aware*
> *Did you not already know*
> *That I was here*

The principal tension lies in the contrast between the sophisticated imagery and twisted syntax of the first three lines and the matter-of-fact fourth line with its slightly archaic omission (in the German) of the main auxiliary verb. This is translated into music as a contrast between the chromatic harmony of the main body of the stanza and the pure and exaggeratedly naïve diatonic harmony of the last line.

The first four bars outline a diminished fourth from F to C-sharp, and the next verse is set to an answering fifth from E down to A.

Dass sie hier gewesen

Op. 59. № 2.

Singstimme. Pianoforte.

Sehr langsam.

Dass der Ostwind Düf_te hau_chet in die Lüf_te,

dadurch thut er _ kund, dass du hier ge_we_sen, dass du hier ge_we_sen.

Dass hier Thränen rin_nen, da _ durch wirst du in_nen,

wär's dir sonst nicht kund, _ dass ich hier ge _ we _ sen, dass ich hier ge_

Although the vocal line of the second part of the phrase is basically diatonic, the accompaniment continues the chromaticism of the opening. The last two lines of the stanza rearrange the notes within these intervals into a new order and expand the fifth to a sixth, from E down to G:

In essence, however, a chromatically harmonized diminished fourth from F to C-sharp is extended downward almost like a resolving response by a diatonic fourth from C-natural to G. "That you were here" is the line with which the present reality breaks in after the scent of the past brought by the east wind, a reality of absence and emptiness; the vocal line only half finishes and the melody in the piano does not finish at all, trailing off onto a dominant seventh chord.

The second stanza repeats the first, with the contrast between chromatic and diatonic harmonies, between the high-pitched diminished fourth and the lower, deliberately commonplace perfect fourth that is part of the outline of a deliberately simple C major chord. This time, however, at the end the piano's melody does not stop but continues its unresolved chord directly into the third stanza, with the strange syntax of the third line and the curious ambiguity of the fourth:

Beauty or love
If remaining hidden?
Perfumes do and tears inform us
That she [it/they] was [were] here

In the third stanza all musical contrasts are blurred and made as ambiguous as the words of the poem. The pure diatonic fourth from C to G is twice transposed upward, and turned into a diminished fifth, from G to C-sharp. Then the diminished fourth from F to C-sharp is changed into a perfect fourth from F to C-natural, first in the piano and then in the voice, and the harmony is diatonic, a dominant seventh of the subdominant—the traditional area in classical eighteenth-century harmony into which one moves when the end of the piece is coming near.

But suddenly with the word "tears" the diatonic atmosphere is made chromatic with a turn to the minor, as the interval from F to C is enlarged in the piano from B-flat to C. Schubert then freely inverts the motif of the refrain *"Dass sie hier gewesen"* with extraordinary effect, and the only real modulation of the song appears with A-flat major to give that simple line a new meaning. The D-flat of A-flat major/F minor turns into the C-sharp of the D minor harmony of the opening (clearly understood throughout as the supertonic minor of C major), and the music returns to the first key.

The song ends with a recall of both the beginning and the end of the first stanza, as if Schubert were realizing in a new way the structure that he affected throughout his life, a strophic pattern in which all the stanzas are set to the same music except for the penultimate one, which makes a dramatic break with the traditional repetition. In the various combinations of the four notes F, E, D, C-sharp that make up the melody of the opening bars no possibility has been omitted: each one of the four is, at some point, followed by, and preceded by, each one of the others. As a result, the melody is less like the working out of a well-defined motif than a small musical space in which objects can be rearranged at will.

The conception of music inherited from Beethoven is radically upset by this technique, and the experience of a formal structure composed by Schubert may be very different from the perception of one of Beethoven's. In a Schubert song, the original motif does not always seem, as in a work by Beethoven, to take on a more substantial form through all of its developments and reappearances but, instead, to be partially dissolved by its transformations and diffused into a larger idiosyncratic space of its own. In this, it resembles the diffusion of Schumann's "Sphinxes" in *Carnaval*. In a work of Beethoven, it is inevitably the original appearance of the motif that is fundamental, while Schumann does not even present his Sphinxes, on which the entire work is based, until the piece is half over. Which of the different versions of Schubert's original four notes in *"Dass sie hier gewesen"* is most basic would be impossible to decide—the chromatic or the diatonic? or one of the other rearrangements? What becomes more substantial in Schubert's song, however, is the process of transformation, the blurring of the opposition between major and minor, chromatic and diatonic. The motif loses its definition as its elements are rearranged, while the attention is focused on the interval that it outlines and on the gradual expansion of this space as the song moves to its conclusion.

It is not only in vocal works that Schubert is able to shift emphasis away from the motif itself to the contour or profile of the space defined by the motif. Like "Du bist die Ruh," the opening movement of the Sonata for Piano in B-flat Major, D. 960, starts with a space defined by four notes, enlarges that space to an augmented fourth, and rearranges and inflects the elements within it. The effect is one of effortless lyricism, apparently static, but building an extraordinary tension by the way the melody is sustained so quietly and within so small a space—the soft trill in the bass is a witness to the suppressed agitation. The energy of Beethoven's motivic technique arises most directly from the repetition of the motif, sometimes merely insistent, often arranged in a rising

[120]

F. S. 107.

sequence: the repetition establishes and confirms its identity. This kind of dynamism is wonderfully prevented at the outset by Schubert. The first two bars present four pitches as a motif of six notes, and this motif will partially dominate the movement. Bars 3 and 4 rearrange the pitches in a different order, and this is the first step toward weakening the motif by blurring its identity. The E-flat at the opening of the fifth bar adds a fifth pitch: even without emphasis, this note has an intense expressive charge merely by its sudden expansion of the tiny space in which the melody has been confined. Bars 5, 6, and 7 continue to find different patterns for the first four notes. This effectively breaks down the motivic identity, and in so doing neutralizes its energy. In this way, Schubert destroys, at least for a moment, one of the sources of the classical technique, the motivic energy that Beethoven had inherited from Haydn and developed to an unprecedented degree.

The counterstatement in bars 10 through 19 continues the work of giving the contour of the melody priority over the motivic construction; it alters the original notes only slightly with a chromatic coloration, and prepares a new counterstatement beginning at bar 20, in which the melody, still pianissimo—all dynamic emphasis repressed until bar 34—finally moves out of its enclosed space, and the harmony leaves the tonic for G-flat major, a tonality for which the groundwork has been subtly laid by the two soft trills in the bass. It is here that the motif of the opening bars becomes at last a source of energy in the classical manner, although the move toward a flat or subdominant key completely evades the emphasis on the dominant area that is traditional at this point of a classical sonata.

In short, Schubert partly exploits and partly refuses the dynamism characteristic of Beethoven that we find even in the elder composer's Adagios. At the opening of this sonata, as in some of the songs, Schubert looks to the interval defined by the melody to give him the basic material he needs for the drama disguised by the lyrical surface. Although he still constructs his melodies with the classical motivic technique, he has learned to eliminate the energy of the motif when he wants to, when the energy would force a dynamic movement too early and too quickly for his sustained line. Many of his most characteristic melodies are no longer impelled from within but shaped by the space that they themselves define.

The treatment of motif in Schubert corresponds to the treatment of tonality in Schumann and Chopin. There are works like Chopin's Ballade No. 2 and Schumann's *Kreisleriana* in which the basic key of the whole piece is not revealed at the outset but only defined progressively as the work proceeds. We do not hear the tonic chord of C major in root position or even the main theme of Schumann's Fan-

tasie in C Major, opus 17, until the last page of the
first movement. If we insist on relying upon a
method of analysis developed strictly for Beethoven,
and especially apt for the tradition from which he
came, we cannot fully appreciate the achievements
of Chopin and Schumann, or even grasp the individual nature of Schubert's style, so different from
Beethoven's, although so close in many ways that
it is difficult to separate at the deepest level.

This may appear at first sight to be an issue of
purely formal and technical description. Nevertheless, it is only by getting the formal aspect right
that we can see how Schubert's music conveys a
different view of experience, and reflects his age in
its attempt to go beyond the rendering of what
might be conceived as the underlying static conditions of appearance—the structure beneath the
skin, so to speak—and to represent instead the very
movement of phenomena. In Europe, after the in-
toxication of the French Revolution, the failure of
so many of its expectations, and the violence of
the succeeding decades, stability was conceived no
longer as a characterless, passive state, as the absence
of turmoil, but as an arbitrary condition imposed
by force and by the exercise of power. For Schubert's
generation, the unspoken faith in a preexisting the-
oretical order that governed and controlled the dis-
order of experience from within was beginning to
weaken. The rapid and confusing succession of

events in contemporary life was not, as before, a surface manifestation of a simpler order and more fundamental laws, moral and divine, but the basis of history and of existence. Theory no longer had any ideal priority over fact: "The factual is already theory," wrote Goethe in *Wilhelm Meisters Wanderjahre*. "The blue of the heavens reveals to us the chromatic law of optics. Only do not look behind the phenomena, they themselves are the doctrine."

Even the most technical description of music will bring us eventually to history. No doubt the relationship between analysis and historical interpretation is reciprocal, a movement back and forth generally called hermeneutic. But the movement is difficult to establish: the relation is most often based on metaphor—a Beethoven symphony is like the French Revolution, for example—and the human mind is so constituted that it will insist on finding a resemblance between any two objects or forms presented for its inspection; and the more unlike the two objects, the more enjoyable is the challenge to discover the secret likeness. The essential condition of music is its proximity to nonsense, its refusal from the outset of a fixed meaning. That is why starting with historical interpretation in order to explain the formal aspects of music is certain disaster: it is too easy to convince ourselves that anything we say is true, and too hard to convince anyone else. Only when the movement back and forth between historical and formal interpretation starts and ends with the music itself do we have any possibility of saying something sensible.

At the end of the eighteenth century, music was the envy of all the other arts because of its refusal to be bound by any rigid system of meaning. The most adventurous writers began to look for ways in which language itself could similarly refuse to be tied down. Georg Christoph Lichtenberg wrote provocatively: "Is there a royal decree that a word must have a fixed meaning?"[21] Even more than literature and the visual arts, music can never be arrested by any system of analysis or interpretation, either formal or historical. It is natural to look outside or beyond the music, to find the ways in which it can temporarily and provisionally assume different kinds of significance. Nevertheless, music will not acknowledge a context greater than itself—social, cultural, or biographical—to which it is conveniently subservient. To paraphrase Goethe's grandiose warning to the scientist: do not look behind the notes, they themselves are the doctrine.

NOTES

1. Prosper de Barante, *Etudes littéraires et historiques* (Paris, 1859), pp. 71–72:

... il n'est pas question ici de savoir, si en rapportant les productions de Schiller à de certaines règles, en les comparant à des formes dont on a le goût et l'habitude, on les trouve bonnes ou mauvaises; chacun là-dessus peut prononcer à sa guise. Se livrer à un tel examen serait une tâche superflue et fort stérile. Au contraire, il peut y avoir quelque avantage à rechercher les rapports que les ouvrages de Schiller ont avec le caractère, la situation et les opinions de l'auteur, et avec les circonstances qui l'ont entouré. La critique, envisagée ainsi, n'a pas un caractère aussi facile et aussi absolu que lorsqu'elle absout ou condamne, d'après la plus ou moins grande ressemblance avec des formes données; mais elle se rapproche davantage de l'étude de l'homme, et de cette observation de l'esprit humain dans sa marche, la plus utile et la plus curieuse de toutes les recherches.

2. *Athenaeum*, Vol. II, p. 285:

Vortreffliche Werke pflegen sich selbst zu charakterisieren und in dieser Rücksicht ist es überflüssig, wenn ein andrer dasselbe Geschäft noch einmal verrichtet, was der Autor ohne Zweifel schon gethan haben wird. Ist eine solche Charakteristik indessen, wie sie es immer seyn sollte, ein Kunstwerk, so ist ihr Dasein zwar nichts weniger als überflüssig, aber sie steht ganz für sich, und ist so unabhängig von der charakterisirten Schrift, wie diese selbst von der in ihr behandelten und gebildeten Materie.

3. See Lewis Lockwood, *Beethoven: Studies in the Creative Process* (Cambridge, Mass., 1992), pp. 167–80.

4. See *The Romantic Generation: The Charles Eliot Norton Lectures 1980–81* (Cambridge, Mass., forthcoming), and "The First Movement of Chopin's Sonata in B♭ minor, opus 35," *Nineteenth-Century Music* (Summer 1990), pp. 60–66.

5. Schumann, *Klavierwerke* (Munich), II, p. 120; bar 200.

6. Charles Burney, *Music, Men, and Manners in France and Italy, 1770* (London, 1969), p. 154.

7. Johann Ernst Wagner, in *Morgenblatt, Wien im Kunst- und Industrie-Comtoir* (July 1807), No. 163: Den verschiedenen Charakter grosser *Tonkünstler* scharf und gründlich aufzufassen, und mit Besonnenheit darzustellen, diess ist—solange die Musik selbst noch träumend zwischen Natur und Idee, und gewisser-maassen zwischen Scheinen und Seyn herumtaumelt— *unmöglich*. Das einzige Mittel, hier und da *etwas Weniges* vom Charakter deutlich zu machen, besteht in Ver-gleichungen der *Tonkünstler* mit *Dichtern*.

8. Ibid.: Wenn wir also z. *B. Haydn* den wahren musikalischen *Wieland* nennen, den verstorbenen *Mozart* in vielen Punkten mit *Schiller'n* vergleichen, oder *van Beethoven*

einige Eigenschaften *Jean Pauls* beylegen, so springt uns—wer kann es läugnen?—plötzlich ein Lichtfunke im Charakter jener Tonkünstler auf.

9. Ibid.:
unstreitig der entschiedenste aller Mollisten ist. Durch seine *Fürchterlichkeit* im Moll, durch ein überall *strenges* System, und eine gewisse philosophische *Korrektheit* bleibt *Mozart* aber dennoch *Schillern* am ähnlichsten, der auch im Moll fast immer als der strengste mit schönen Hoffnungen für die Zukunft. —Der Uebergang zum ersten Theile—wobey das zweyte Horn furchtsam das Thema zu probiren oder *darzubieten* scheint, welches nun alle Instrumente, Fortissimo, und in einem ungeheuern Triller sich vereinigend, schnell wieder *aufzunehmen beschliessen*—hat wohl an Herrlichkeit schwerlich seines Gleichen. Der erste scheinbare Schluss, welchen ein grosser überraschender *Orgelgriff* wieder zerstört, und die nun allmählig sich vorbereitende und heranschwellende *Füllung* mit dem blossen Thema, bis zum gewaltigsten himmlischen Zusammenklang im höhern Chor—alles diess, in einer ganz neuen Art von Kirchenstyl ausgeführt, reisst endlich mit wunderbarer Macht die Thore des Herzens auf, und erfüllt uns mit unsäglichem Erstaunen.

10. Jean Paul Richter, *Flegeljahre* (1804–5), Book II, No. 26, para. 1.
Nun glomm ein schwacher Funke zum nachherigen Kriegsfeuer schon unter dem Essendurch das einzige Wort an, dass ein Deutscher von einem deutschen grossen Dreiklang sprach, worin Haydn, sagt' er, den Aeschylus, Gluck den Sophokles, Mozart den Euripides vorstelle. Ein anderer sagte, von Gluck geb' ers

zu, aber Mozart sei der Shakespeare. Jetzt mengten
sich die Italier darein, zu Ehren des Kappelmeisters,
und sagten, in Neapel geige man dem Mozart was.

11. See Ludwig Tieck, *Phantasus* (1812), last pages of
Part I.

12. Ibid.:
Schon früher war es für mich eine Epoche meines Le-
bens gewesen, diesen alten wahren Gesang kennen zu
lernen: ich hatte immer nach Musik, nach der höch-
sten, gedürstet, und geglaubt, keinen Sinn für diese
Kunst zu besitzen, als mit der Kenntnis des Palestrina,
Leo, Allegri, und jener Alten, die man jetzt von den
Liebhabern selten oder nie nennen hört, mein Gehör
und mein Geist erwachte . . . Seitdem glaube ich
eingesehen zu haben, dass nur dieses die wahre Musik
sei, und dass der Strom, den man in den weltlichen
Luxus unserer Oper hinein geleitet hat, um ihn mit
Zorn, Rache und allen Leidenschaften zu versetzen,
trübe und unlauter geworden ist: denn unter den Kün-
sten ist die Musik die religiöseste, sie ist ganz Andacht,
Sehnsucht, Demut, Liebe; sie kann nicht pathetisch
sein, und auf ihre Stärke und Kraft pochen, oder sich
in Verzweiflung austoben wollen, hier verliert sie ihren
Geist, und wird nur eine schwache Nachahmerin der
Rede und Poesie.

13. Ibid.:
Nur muss man mich kein Requiem von ihm wollen
hören lassen, oder mich zu überzeugen suchen, dass
er, so wie die meisten Neueren, wirklich eine geistliche
Musik habe setzen können.

14. Ibid.:

Himmel und Hölle, die durch unermessliche Klüfte getrennt waren, sind zauberhaft und zum Erschrecken in der Kunst vereinigt, die ursprünglich reines Licht, stille Liebe und lobpreisende Andacht war. So erscheint mir Mozarts Musik.

Es war den neusten Zeiten vorbehalten, fuhr Lothar fort, den wundervollen Reichtum des menschlichen Sinnes in dieser Kunst, vorzüglich in der Instrumental-Musik auszusprechen.

15. Ibid.:

Und wie es dem Menschen allenthalben geschieht, wenn er alle Schranken überfliegen und das Letzte und Höchste erringen will, dass die Leidenschaft in sich selbst zerbricht und zersplittert, das Gegenteil ihrer ursprünglichen Grösse, so geschieht es auch wohl in dieser Kunst grossen Talenten. Wenn wir Mozart wahnsinnig nennen dürfen, so ist der genialische Beethoven oft nicht vom Rasenden zu unterscheiden, der selten einen musikalischen Gedanken verfolgt und sich in ihm beruhigt, sondern durch die gewalttätigsten Übergänge springt und der Phantasie gleichsam selbst im rastlosen Kampfe zu entfliehen sucht.

Alle diese neuen tiefsinnigen Bestrebungen, sagte Anton, sind meinem Gemüte nicht fremd, sie tönen wie das Rauschen des Lebensstromes zwischen Felsen-ufern, der über Klippen und hemmendem Gestein in romantischer Wildnis musikalisch braust; nur das ist mir unbegreiflich geblieben, wie die Schöpfung und die Tageszeiten unsers Haydn fast allenthalben haben Glück machen können, deren kindische Malerei gegen allen höheren Sinn streitet. Seine Symphonien und

Instrumental-Kompositionen sind meist so vortref-
flich, dass man ihm diese Verirrung niemals hätte zu-
trauen sollen.

16. Karl Ditters von Dittersdorff, *Memoirs*:
Er ist unstreitig eins der grössten Originalgenies, und
ich habe bisher noch keinen Komponisten gekannt,
der so einen erstaunlichen Reichtum von Gedanken
besitzt. Ich wünschte, er wäre nicht so verschwende-
risch damit. Er lässt den Zuhörer nicht zu Atem kom-
men; denn, kaum will man einem schönen Gedanken
nachsinnen, so steht schon wieder ein anderer herr-
licher da, der den vorigen verdrängt, und das geht
immer in einem so fort, so dass man am Ende keine
dieser Schönheiten im Gedächtnis aufbewahren kann.

17. Otto von Loeben, in *Sämtliche Werke des Freiherrn
Joseph von Eichendorff*, XIII: *Briefe an Eichendorff*,
Wilhelm Kosch, ed. (Regensburg), p. 19.

18. Johann Friedrich Reichardt, *Vertraute Briefe auf einer
Reise nach Wien . . .* (1810).

19. Burney, *Music, Men, and Manners in France and Italy*,
pp. 89, 98.

20. Goethe to Zelter:
. . . Beethoven habe ich in Töpliz kennen gelernt.
Sein Talent hat mich in Erstaunen gesetzt; allein er ist
leider eine ganz unbändige Persönlichkeit, die zwar
nicht Unrecht hat, wenn sie die Welt detestabel findet,
aber sie freilich dadurch weder für sich noch für andere
genussreicher macht. Sehr zu entschuldigen ist er hin-
gegen und sehr zu bedauern, da ihn sein Gehör verlässt,
das vielleicht dem musikalischen Teil seines Wesens
weniger als dem geselligen schadet. Er, der ohnehin

lakonischer Natur ist, wird es nun doppelt durch diesen
Mangel . . .

Zelter to Goethe:
   Berlin, 14 September 1812
Was Sie von Bethofen sagen ist ganz natürlich. Auch
ich bewundere ihn mit Schrecken. Seine eigene Werke
seinen ihm heimliches Grauen zu verursachen. Eine
Empfindung die in der neuen Kultur viel zu leicht-
sinnig beseitigt wird. Mir erscheinen seine Werke wie
Kinder deren Vater ein Weib oder Mutter ein Mann
wäre. Das Letzte mir bekannt gewordne Werk (Chri-
stus am Ölberg) kommt mir vor wie eine Unkeusch-
heit, deren Grund und Ziel ein ewiger Tod ist. Die
musikal. Kritiker, welche sich alles besser zu verstehn
scheinen als auf Naturell und Eigentümlichkeit, haben
sich auf die seltsamste Weise in Lob und Tadel über
diesen Komponisten ergossen. Ich kenne musikal.
Personen, die sich sonst bei Anhörung seiner Werke
alarmiert ja indigniert fanden und nun von einer Leidenschaft dafür ergriffen sind, wie die Anhänger der
griechischen Liebe. Wie wohl man sich dabei befinden
kann lässt sich begreifen und was daraus entstehn kann,
haben Sie in den Wahlverwandschaften deutlich genug
gezeigt.

21. Georg Christoph Lichtenberg, *Notebook E*, No. 85.

INDEX

INDEX

TEIKYO WESTMAR UNIV. LIBRARY

ML 3845 .R68 1994
Rosen, Charles, 1927-
The frontiers of meaning
                (94-1924)

DEMCO